Communication and Economic Life

For Max and Ezra

Communication and Economic Life

LIZ MOOR

polity

First published in 2022 by Polity Press

Polity Press
65 Bridge Street
Cambridge CB2 1UR, UK

Polity Press
101 Station Landing
Suite 300
Medford, MA 02155, USA

ISBN-13: 978-0-7456-8701-8
ISBN-13: 978-0-7456-8702-5(pb)

A catalogue record for this book is available from the British Library.

Library of Congress Control Number: 2021939063

Typeset in 11.25 on 13 Dante
by Fakenham Prepress Solutions, Fakenham, Norfolk NR21 8NL
Printed and bound in Great Britain by CPI Group (UK) Ltd, Croydon

The publisher has used its best endeavours to ensure that the URLs for external websites referred to in this book are correct and active at the time of going to press. However, the publisher has no responsibility for the websites and can make no guarantee that a site will remain live or that the content is or will remain appropriate.

For further information on Polity, visit our website:
politybooks.com

Contents

Acknowledgements

Many people have helped me to complete this book. Three reviewers of the original proposal made helpful suggestions, while Nick Couldry, Jo Littler and Don Slater offered early encouragement. Parts of chapter 1 were presented to the Geography department at the University of Nottingham and I greatly appreciated their attentive reading and thoughtful comments. Some ideas were also tested at a MeCCSA panel organized by Rebecca Bramall, who has been kind and supportive throughout. At Polity, Stephanie Homer, Ellen MacDonald-Kramer and Mary Savigar have all been endlessly patient and accommodating, for which I am very grateful.

Friends and colleagues who read parts of the text include Clea Bourne, Beckie Coleman, David Moats and Dave O'Brien. I would like to thank them for their frank and constructive feedback. The remaining errors and omissions are my own.

Some parts of chapter 2 have previously been published in *Consumption, Markets and Culture* and in the *Journal of Cultural Economy*. I am grateful to Jonathan Schroeder for encouraging me to put my thoughts about money symbolism down on paper at a relatively early stage, and to Liz McFall for ongoing enthusiasm and kindness. Liz has been central to many people's experience of intellectual community in recent years, at a time when it has been especially important. My thinking about price (and much else) has been enriched through conversations with Celia Lury. Lana Swartz provided encouragement and inspiration from across the Atlantic.

Colleagues at Goldsmiths supported me with a one-term sabbatical. I am particularly grateful to Clea Bourne, Natalie Fenton, Gholam Khiabany, Rachel Moore, Anamik Saha, Gareth Stanton and Milly Williamson for encouragement, gifts of books and cakes, teaching and administrative cover, and general good vibes. I would also like to thank Jenny Carpenter, Sam Friedman, Meghan Horvath, Shireen Kanji, Kate Maclean, Rebecca Strong and Emma Uprichard. Chris Arning made trips to the British Library more companionable. Max and Ezra are the best possible people to come home to. Special thanks to Sarah Bloomfield for the expert childcare that made finishing the book possible.

Introduction

At the end of 2016, Anand Menon, an expert on European politics, reflected on what he had learned from a year spent travelling around the UK to discuss the referendum on leaving the European Union. During a trip to the northeast of England he had told a town hall-style meeting that the vast majority of economists agreed that exiting the EU would lead to a substantial economic slowdown, and a two per cent drop in gross domestic product (or GDP), the usual measure of an economy's health. Responding to him, a member of the audience had shouted, 'That's your bloody GDP. Not ours!'. On another excursion, he had met a woman in Yorkshire who told him that she didn't mind taking the economic 'hit' associated with Brexit, but that it would be 'nice to see the rich folk down south suffer' (Menon 2016a). Reflecting on these events, Menon thought that they showed a distrust of elites and experts, but also a distrust of aggregate data and statistics. Perhaps it was all very well to show that *on average* membership of the EU had increased GDP, or that *on average* migration to the UK had been positive for the economy, but if these averages did not tally with people's own experience, then it was unsurprising that the figures might not seem to 'belong' to them (Menon 2016b). As one commentator observed, maybe Menon's heckler was right that the UK economy had become so unequal that 'it can no longer be talked about as one unitary economy' (Chakrabortty 2017).

Academic research confirms that not everyone experiences the economy in the same way, and that many people struggle to understand key concepts. When Jack Mosse (2018) asked people in north London to define 'the economy', most were unable to do so, and when he asked them if they felt part of it, many simply didn't understand what he meant. It is not just that measures like GDP reflect national rather than local output, but that the terms themselves – sometimes even terms like 'the economy' – are often too far from most people's experience to be meaningful. There is a split between the breadth of our actual economic lives and what counts as the economy in more formal spaces. This is reflected in my own discipline of media and communications. When we talk about media and the economy, 'the economy' is usually understood as the macro economy or the activities included in GDP, and 'the media' usually refers to television and print news, or the websites and social media feeds of news providers.[1] Alternatively, we may think about how patterns of ownership or other business relationships influence 'communication', but this is understood almost exclusively in terms of the *mass* communication of news or advertising, rather than the way people talk in everyday life. While work in this field has been very good at showing how few voices get heard in news reporting of economic crises (e.g., Berry 2013) or how 'bad' economic news tends to attract more coverage than good (Harrington 1989; Damstra and Boukes 2021), it has mostly avoided questioning how concepts of 'the economy' are arrived at in the first place, and who or what this leaves out.

The importance of economic *communication*, when it is addressed, is understood either in terms of comprehension or in terms of 'bias'. In the wake of the global financial crisis of 2008, for example, public debate focused partly on the question of why no one had seemed to see it coming, but also on the extent to which the language of finance, as well as the financial products being described, had become so complex that few people, including regulators, could understand it (see, e.g., GAO 2009; Schwarcz 2009). As John Lanchester, a novelist and chronicler of the crisis, put it some years later, 'the language of money is a powerful tool, and it is also a tool of power. Incomprehension is a form of consent. If we allow ourselves not to understand this language, we are signing off on the way the world works today' (2014: n.p.). In this view, many of the problems of the financial sector were really problems of communication and comprehension. The solution was something like a collective education programme: Lanchester encouraged those who shared his concerns to learn the language of finance so that they may better scrutinize the financial sector and hold it to account.

Learning the language of finance may not be for everyone, but Lanchester nonetheless captured something important about the gap between the language of economics on the one hand, and the economic experiences of ordinary people on the other. This gap has been observed since at least Hayek's time: he lamented the domination of economics by mathematics and statistics, and the tendency of economists to adopt a 'scientistic' tone that gave special significance to 'numerical statements and quantitative measurements' (1942: 275). For him, this took economists too far away from the attempt to understand the human and subjective groundings of economic action. In recent years, however, this criticism has taken on a new significance, as those with an undergraduate degree in economics, or related subjects such as accounting, have come to occupy a growing proportion of senior roles in the civil service (in contrast to the earlier dominance of classics and the humanities), as well as more broadly in government and public life (Davis 2017: 598–9). The consequence, some suggest, is a serious knowledge gap between those in power and those they represent, on questions that have a material effect on their lives.

Problems of comprehension are also blamed on 'the media', and particularly those media organizations with a public service remit. Criticism of their role in economic communication typically takes two forms. The first, which often comes from media and communication researchers, is that there is a bias or skew in the selection of viewpoints and speakers that feature in coverage of economic issues. In the UK, early studies of media coverage of the economy found a tendency to replicate dominant narratives and framings (Eldridge 1995), while more recent studies have found that many mainstream discussions of economic matters privilege voices from business over either academic economists or the representatives of workers and unions (e.g., Berry 2016a). A second criticism, arguably even more powerful, is that national media, including public service media, often fail to *explain* economic debates in ways that are accessible to a wide audience. This in turn reinforces, rather than reduces, the gap in understanding between the public and those in power (or those with a background in business and finance). Consider the findings of two surveys from 2015 and 2016: in one, 60 per cent of adults in the UK could not identify the correct definition of GDP from a multiple choice, and almost half could not identify the correct definition of the government budget deficit, yet only a tiny number described the subject as 'unimportant'. In another, only 12 per cent of respondents agreed that 'politicians and the media tend to talk about economics in an accessible way that makes it easy to understand' (Inman 2015; YouGov 2016). Taken together, this lack of understanding of key concepts, and the widespread sense that neither governments nor media organizations are especially willing to explain them, means that only those with existing knowledge are able to take something useful – or even comprehensible – from economic news coverage. This has unfortunate implications for democratic participation, since it makes it much harder to evaluate politicians' claims about the country's economic situation, or their proposals for future action. And faced with large volumes of hard-to-parse information, it may be more tempting to rely on 'gut instinct' – something that can easily be manipulated by politicians (see, e.g., Andrejevic 2013; Davies 2018a).

Both criticisms have merit, and both turn on the claim that, one way or another, media are not just reporting on reality but shaping it – either through a heavy-handed or partial framing of issues, or by neglecting the educational or explanatory dimensions of their role. But I want to suggest a third way in which media shape reality, which is through their definition of 'the economy' itself. The claim of this book is that there is in fact a lot more to economic life and economic communication than the contents of the business, financial and economics sections of newspapers or television news, and that while the language of economics and the media reporting of economic issues are vitally important areas of research and study, they should not be seen as coextensive with the economic lives of most people. Many people find it hard to see their own lives reflected in either the official language of economics or the way economic matters are reported on television, but this is partly because the definitions of 'the economy' in these places are so limited. What is more, these limitations are often replicated in academic studies of economic communication. When this happens, social science disciplines make it harder rather than easier for people to understand the connections between 'the patterns of their own lives and the course of world history' (Mills 1959: 4).

In what follows, I attempt to challenge these narrow definitions of the economic, and expand our horizon away from news and current affairs. Instead, I propose a framework for thinking about economic communication that foregrounds the broader category of *communicative practices* rather than 'media', and that understands economic life not only in terms of the macro economy and GDP, but more sociologically as a set of processes of providing for material wants and needs, which may be subjectively meaningful for those engaged in them (Weber 1978). To do this, I first highlight how economic action *itself* is communicative, and then explore how our economic lives are constructed communicatively in a variety of modes that move through, but also exceed, mass media. The modalities that I focus on in Part II of the book – promotion, information, narrative and discussion – remind us not only that 'the economy' looks different in different communicative practices, but also that the values governing economic life are not so uniform as they sometimes seem. A communicative practice like 'informing', discussed in chapter 4, may have two quite different sets of meanings: one that is relatively open, and has to do with disseminating facts and ideas; another that is more secretive and involves passing information to those in power. Discussions online often challenge the accounts of economic life offered by banks or even schools, and the economic narratives found in films and novels, discussed in chapter 5, often reflect quite different value systems from those found in television news or newspapers' financial pages. This plurality of values matters, because it is part of what makes economic change thinkable.

In the remainder of this introduction I outline the frameworks and theoretical ideas that underpin the chapters that follow, and the account of communication and economic life that the book offers: first, I explore the idea that 'the economy' is a historical construction, rather than natural category, and the consequences of this for social science researchers; next, I outline the rationale for starting from a conception of 'communication' or 'communicative practices' rather than 'media'; finally, I explain why it is appropriate to assume value plurality in economic life.

The economy and 'economic life'

In arguing that media researchers would benefit from a new way of thinking about communication and economic life, I am suggesting, first of all, that they need a way of framing 'the economy' that does not depend solely on the definitions used by governments, or the range of topics designated as 'economic' by television news. The first step, therefore, is to recognize all the ways in which the economy, as an object of study, is already constructed, even before its appearance in media. Michael Emmison (1983) has shown that modern uses of the term 'economy' did not appear until the 1930s, alongside Keynes's conception of the macro economy and his proposal of a wider role for government in managing it. More recently, Timothy Mitchell has shown that the modern Western concept of 'the economy' – in the sense of 'the structure or totality of relations of production, distribution and consumption of goods and services within a given country or region' (1998: 84) – emerged with the shift from colonial government to a post-colonial world order, and partly as an outgrowth of the experience of colonial rule (Mitchell 2002: 83–4). Here, 'the economy' appears at the intersection of various new forms of discourse, techniques of measurement and forms of classification, including maps that link territories to ownership, and statistics that capture information about populations and their assets.

Perhaps the most influential definition of 'the economy' and economic activity is gross domestic product (GDP). In recent years it, too, has become an object of some scrutiny. This is because the way it is calculated leaves out various activities that might legitimately be seen as 'economic' while overstating the significance of others. These decisions have important consequences, because they reinforce a sense of what is productive and therefore valuable and, by implication, what is not. Diane Coyle's (2014) study of the history of GDP shows that one important omission is household production. Work based in the home, including caring work and cleaning work, is not included in GDP measures because it is unpaid, despite the fact that it is clearly both productive and valuable (indeed its value can readily be estimated through reference to its paid equivalent). Its omission means that much work – often women's work – is in effect considered unproductive. Similarly, many digital goods and services (including Google, Wikipedia, Twitter) that contribute to economic welfare are not included in GDP because they are zero-priced, intangible and often hard to measure. Yet they are surely productive and valuable. This is a problem for economists, as Coyle notes, because it makes the gap between economic welfare – i.e., general living standards, prosperity and wellbeing – and the definition of economic output unhelpfully wide.[2] But there is also a salutary lesson here for researchers in other fields who take formal definitions of 'the economy' at face value, thereby consigning certain aspects of productive experience to some other domain of study altogether.

The consequences of relying on narrow definitions of 'the economy' for media and other social science research can also be illustrated by another example from Coyle's work, to do with the role of finance. The value of the financial sector to the national economy has been overestimated by between one fifth and one half, according to Coyle, in large part because of a controversial change to the calculation of GDP that allowed financial risk-taking to be counted as an 'output' rather than an intermediate service, which would not normally be included. Where previous accounting techniques showed financial services making either a negative, or only barely positive, contribution to GDP, the methodological change 'turned finance from a conceptually unproductive into a productive sector' (2014: 103, 104). This had significant political effects. As Coyle shows, the view that finance is a strategically important sector of the economy developed alongside those statistical changes, but a belief in finance's strategic importance made it more likely that regulatory reform would be shaped around it in beneficial and supportive ways. The problem for media research is that the classifications and definitions of 'the economy' used by government agencies tend to get repeated in news and current affairs,[3] and then, by extension, by media researchers themselves. The pages of media and communications journals show fairly clearly how much more importance the discipline attaches to finance than, for example, housework or care work.[4] This does not mean that finance is unimportant – indeed there would be good reasons to study it even if it were seen as *un*productive through the lens of GDP – but it does show how much ordinary economic action might be deemed irrelevant if we follow government or media definitions of economic life to the exclusion of all others.

How might media researchers avoid relying on definitions of the economy that either exclude important aspects of productive activity or simply replicate the choices of news editors? There are at least two ways to do so. The first would be to recognize that 'the economy' is the outcome of a process – often conflicted or contested – and then to shift more attention to that process, rather than its outcome. The process, following Çalişkan and Callon (2009, 2010), might be called 'economization'. This refers to all the ways in which 'activities, behaviours and spheres or fields are established as being economic' (2009: 370). In the same way that social researchers see 'the social' as a constant production (Hall 1977; see also Couldry 2006: 17), so, too, is the economy 'an achievement rather than a starting point or pre-existing reality' (Çalişkan and Callon 2009: 370). One now well-established way of looking at processes of economization is to focus on the work of economists, and the field of economics, since these actors are often a powerful influence on how real-life economies and markets are made, as well as being key voices within government. I take up this idea in chapter 1, where I look at the way economists have historically downplayed the role of communication in economic life, or else skewed its definition towards 'information'.

A second way to avoid 'capture' by governmental or media definitions of the economy is to more explicitly incorporate anthropological and sociological understandings of economic life into our definitions of the field of study. For both sociologists and anthropologists, what is of interest is not so much 'the economy' itself as some pre-given thing, but rather 'economic action' as a purposive activity. And economic action, in turn, is interesting because of its *meaningfulness* for those involved and its continuity with other forms of social action (Weber 1978). The first part of this argument concerns the scope of 'the economic'. In Weber's account of economy and society, actions were 'economically oriented' insofar as they were concerned with making provisions or satisfying a desire for utilities (Swedberg 2011). One way of doing this would be via exchange on the market. But households – which were the dominant economic form for much of history – could make provisions for themselves in all kinds of ways, including through home production, non-market exchange and various other forms of production and distribution. Similarly, anthropologists have historically found that economic actions are organized according to logics of reciprocity and redistribution as well as market exchange. This range of forms of provisioning can still be observed today, even in highly specialized market economies where non-market provisioning is assumed to be a minor part of economic activity (and where it is not counted in standard measures of 'the economy'). And yet to focus on 'provisioning' or 'satisfying the desire for utilities' is to imagine a much broader terrain of study – and one that more closely captures everyday experiences of economic life – than either the macro economy or the economics of particular sectors.

The second point concerns the meaningfulness of economic action and its continuity with other forms of action. Weber's economic sociology is again relevant because of his distinction between formal and substantive rationality. In economic action, something is substantively rational to the extent that 'the provisioning of different groups of persons ... is shaped by economically oriented social action under *some criterion (past, present, or potential) of ultimate values*, regardless of the nature of these ends' (cited in Swedberg 2011: 68, emphasis added; see also Weber 1978: 28–30). This is contrasted with a 'formal' economic rationality – of the kind usually modelled by economists – concerned with quantitative calculation of means and ends. As Çalişkan and Callon (2009: 374) note, to adopt a formalist approach to the economy in a field like anthropology (or indeed media studies) is essentially to engage in 'the continuation of economics by other disciplinary means', because it replicates economists' definitions of the terms and purpose of the field of study. A more properly socio-logical or anthropological approach is one that engages with ultimate values and emphasizes the fact that much of what we call 'economic action' is, at some fundamental level, continuous with other kinds of social action. This might mean looking beyond traditional topics (e.g., firms, hiring practices, price setting and market design) to things like student loans, therapy bills, art galleries and branding practices. But the emphasis on the meaningfulness of economic action has also led sociologists after Weber to be much more interested in where the desire for particular 'utilities' comes from, or how the various means chosen to meet and satisfy those needs and preferences come to be socially meaningful rather than simply efficient or functional. Perhaps the most well-known example of this approach comes from Viviana Zelizer (e.g., 1994, 2005), whose work has been concerned not only with the way people combine intimate relationships with economic ones, but also with the way that economic transactions can be used to organize and comment on social relationships. But this approach to the social meaningfulness of economic action can also be seen in Daniel Miller's longstanding insistence (e.g., 1987, 1998, 2001) that the meaning of consumption and provisioning cannot be simply read off from the mode of production within which goods were produced.[5]

I will draw out the implications of these sociological and anthropological definitions of the economy for media researchers in more detail in the conclusion, where I outline some of the potential sites for a reconfigured approach to communication and economic life. In the rest of the book, I draw most explicitly on these insights in chapter 2, where I offer a preliminary account of the symbolic or communicative dimensions of relatively mundane aspects of economic activity (such as payment) and artefacts (such as monetary tokens and prices). Sociological accounts also influence the choice of examples in later chapters – the focus on, for example, debt discussion boards, small-scale investor clubs, online reviews and ratings or audience discussion shows are all ways of emphasizing forms of provisioning and the way these are communicated or mediated, rather than 'the economy' and how it appears in news and current affairs. Finally, I draw on these fields throughout the book in my use of the term 'economic life' rather than 'the economy' (see, e.g., Spillman 2011; Wherry 2012). To focus on economic life is to deliberately distance oneself from definitions of 'the economy' as only the macro economy, and to attempt instead to capture the breadth and diversity of economic activity, beyond capitalism, and even beyond markets (Gibson-Graham 1996, 2006). Instead, it takes as its objects of study those processes of provisioning where both 'economic' and non-economic values collide, mingle and influence each other, and in which the meaning-making activities of ordinary people are as important as the calculating activities of more powerful institutional actors.

Communication, media and economic life

The book's focus on communication and economic life is motivated not only by this expanded conception of 'the economic', but also by a particular approach to media and communication. Media and communications research is a broad field, with many different kinds of scholarship, but in Britain it has historically been concerned primarily with *media* texts, institutions and technologies rather than with the more obvious – and much larger – category of *communication* and communicative practice. This is no doubt partly due to its coexistence alongside a powerful cultural studies tradition, in which the idea of 'communication as culture' (e.g., Carey 1989) has been well developed, and in which there is correspondingly a wider sense of what counts as 'media' for communicative practice.

However, to the extent that media and communications has an identifiable sub-field of *economic* communication, it has been overwhelmingly focused on the way that 'the economy' (understood in the limited ways outlined above) is represented in *media* texts or genres such as 'the news' and, less commonly, film and television. As such, it has tended to overlook a broader range of ways that economic activities, practices and beliefs are constituted communicatively.

Why does a focus on (usually mass) media texts and institutions, rather than a wider array of communicative practices, matter? One reason is simply that it leaves out a great many empirically interesting and consequential aspects of how economic life is constructed communicatively. These include the way people talk about economic matters to family, friends and partners, the way they use computers or phones to research goods or make financial plans, what they learn about money from reading books and magazines, or from watching plays, the way they present themselves at work, the way they choose a hairdresser or how they decide when to make a meal from scratch rather than buy it from a supermarket or restaurant. It also ignores a good deal of the communicative activity that goes on inside businesses and firms, such as meeting, reviewing, complaining or gossiping. As we have seen above, leaving such practices out of our accounts of economic communication may also mean replicating dominant definitions of 'the economy', rather than understanding that these definitions are contested, or the outcome of a process. It also means ignoring the wider sociological and anthropological traditions that explore the symbolic dimensions of economic life and its subjective meaningfulness for those who participate in it.

Another reason to avoid a sole focus on mass media texts such as news is that it leaves the field open to the charge of media-centrism. As Nick Couldry notes, this is a real problem for media and communications scholars because, by assuming the importance of media, we bypass the question of 'how central media *actually are* to the explanation of contemporary change' (Couldry 2006: 12, emphasis added), and ignore the possibility that 'sometimes, perhaps more often than … we suspect, media are *less* consequential in the social world than other forces'. What Couldry has in mind here are broader social and economic forces, including shifts in income, changing patterns of employment or ownership, and so on. But his point remains true even *within* the field of media and communications. There is a tendency to assume that (mass) mediated communications are the most consequential forms of communication, and then to focus on them. Yet the fact of being 'media' or 'mediated' may often be less important than the fact of taking narrative form, or of being a work of science fiction. Of course, the communicative aspects of economic life may ultimately be less important than its other parts too – the extent to which communication *constitutes* economic life is clearly an empirical question – but 'communication' offers a much broader starting point than 'media' (particularly when 'media' is really code for *mass* media texts), and, for scholars interested in these questions, it makes sense to start with them before assessing the extent to which mediation matters.

In practice, focusing on 'economic communication' or 'communication in economic life' means drawing multiple traditions of work into the same orbit. Work on the way that, for example, financial crises or industrial disputes are represented in 'the media' (whether that is news and current affairs, or Hollywood films) must sit alongside work considering how ordinary people discuss debt and savings on internet discussion boards, or how they use savings apps on their phones, but also how their views of capitalism might be formed through reading particular kinds of novels or playing particular kinds of computer games. These are all forms of economic communication, and one is not more 'authentically' economic because it deals with inflation or central bank lending. Within such a framing, *mediation* would be posed as both a question and a spectrum. It has to be a question, rather than something we assume, because not all forms of economic communication are mediated, and certainly not through 'mass' media. As we shall see in chapter 6, the ordinary face-to-face discussions people have about the economy are vital for understanding how people make their own process of provisioning subjectively meaningful, and one of the advantages of attending to them is that they often show how far ordinary understandings of 'the economy' converge with or diverge from accounts offered by either governments or news media. On the other hand, mediation is also a spectrum because as we see in chapters 5 and 6, the 'mediated' versions of these conversations (for example as they take place on internet discussion forums) may share a good deal of the substance of their face-to-face counterparts. Where they differ is that mediated discourse extends the availability of these discussions in time and space, and offers a wider range of interlocutors (and perhaps of viewpoints) than are typically available in everyday life. Studying them alongside each other thus allows us to draw certain conclusions about how much difference mediation makes.

The approach to mediation in the chapters that follow draws on two traditions. The first is the expanded sense of media as including materials, technologies and systems. In this view, communicative forms such as novels, paintings and graffiti might be considered as mediators, because they play a role in shaping how we think about things (they 'get in between' us and some more direct view of a topic or event). But they are also *mediated* in the sense that their communication occurs via materials that place certain limits on them. In fact, all kinds of phenomena can perform a 'mediating' function: trains, radio signals and cloud storage can link people together, and have the potential to enable (but also place limits on) actions that are communicative (Innis 1950; Peters 2015). German sociologists Jurgen Habermas and Niklas Luhmann both include 'money' and 'power' in their definitions of communications media, and Luhmann even includes 'scientific knowledge, art, love, [and] morals' (Fuchs 2011: 90). These are beyond my scope here, but I do take this view of media as materials and systems seriously, particularly in chapter 2, where I look at the symbolic dimensions of money and payments media, and in chapter 3, where I explore the significance of 'delinguistified' and ambient forms of promotion.

The second tradition I draw upon is work in European media studies about 'mediation' or 'mediatization'. This work explores the way that mediated communication creates 'new forms of action and interaction in the social world, new kinds of social relationship and new ways of relating to others and to oneself' (Thompson 1995: 4), and, as an unavoidable part of this, new ways of exercising power. This approach is developed by scholars who argue that the traditional focus of media and communications research – 'mass' communication, separated into the study of production, texts and reception – risks ignoring the significance of a more overarching set of historical developments in which media and processes of mediation have entered into many more aspects of daily life (see, e.g., Livingstone 2009; Couldry and Hepp 2013). In a post-internet age – but discernible before then – it has become much harder to speak about *the* media, as though that referred to a fixed set of forms and genres. Instead, we must begin by acknowledging the mediation, or potential mediation, of many elements of our experience, from taking out a loan or buying a book to going on holiday or seeking advice. From here, we can ask what difference this makes to social interaction and organization, to the distribution of resources, and so on. As various authors have noted, the concept of mediatization is therefore less a grand theoretical framework than a historical claim, a 'sensitizing concept' (Couldry and Hepp 2013) alerting us to what we must now consider when we explore the relationship between media and the social. The concepts of mediation and mediatization are valuable to the study of economic communication because they take seriously the fact that mediation, and mediated messages, can now be found in all kinds of places beyond what we think of as 'the' media, without determining in advance which are likely to be most consequential.

What does all this mean for the study of economic communication and the construction of economic life? I take economic communication to refer to a large, but still circumscribed, set of actions, interactions, encounters and forms of expression, which may be mediated or unmediated (or involve a complex interplay between the two), and which have to do, very broadly, with ways of understanding and providing for our material wants and needs. As I have suggested, a major theme of the rest of the book concerns the role played by both communication, broadly understood, as well as specific media technologies in defining the content, scope and limits of 'the economic', both as an object out there in the world (as, for example, in the case of the construction of the economy on television news) and as a lived set of experiences of provisioning.

Value plurality in economic life

A final concept underpinning the rest of the book is that of *value plurality*. If we take seriously the expanded view of economic communication outlined above – that is, if we are willing to include novels, films, social media accounts or online forum discussions as instances of economic communication – then we will likely find that economic life is marked by a much wider range of ideas, values and beliefs than if we focused solely on the way that 'the economy', understood in conventional terms as the macro economy and particular industrial sectors, is represented on television and in the press. We may live in societies dominated by capitalist logics and forms of accumulation, or that depend on consumer spending for growth, but to believe in value plurality is to believe that our material circumstances do not necessarily exhaust our ways of thinking about the world. In much of what follows, therefore, I keep 'value plurality' as an open question: to what extent do particular modes of economic communication (e.g., promoting, informing, narrating), media (e.g., books, films) or genres (e.g., news, advice, self-help) imply or invoke particular sets of values, or particular ways of framing and constructing economic life?

In foregrounding this question, I am drawing on a tradition of thought, spread across various social science disciplines, that sees economic life as governed by multiple logics, rather than a single capitalist logic. Within this tradition, we might start by considering Nick Couldry's (2006) work on the 'myth of the mediated centre', mentioned above. In challenging the idea that media are our privileged points of access to social reality or shared social values, Couldry notes that while there may be a bureaucratic or organizational centre to social life, there may not necessarily be any 'centre' of social values at all. Rhetorical claims about 'the nation', or 'society', are often rhetorical only, and the coherence or otherwise of social values is something to investigate empirically, rather than to assume. Indeed, if we look closely, he suggests, we might see 'disorder or a lesser degree of order: disputes over value, contests over legitimacy, [and] alternative explanations of social change' (2006: 16). In making this argument, Couldry is drawing in part on earlier challenges to the idea of a 'dominant ideology' (e.g., Abercrombie et al. 1981). In this critique, the claim that an ideological 'glue' or superstructure is necessary to hold capitalist societies together in the face of their internal contradictions is wrong, simply because it overlooks the sheer range of other things that might make societies cohere. People may not accept the versions of social reality offered by a dominant class, or found in mainstream media output, but are often too busy with work and making ends meet to 'resist' in any way that critics would recognize. In any case, ideological control, or even consent, may not be necessary for the status quo to survive; it may indeed be the *diversity* of views and plurality of belief systems that keeps the organizational centre relatively stable.

The idea that economic life may be governed by multiple logics can also be traced in Boltanski and Thévenot's (2006) notion of competing orders of worth. In their work they find 'critical tensions ... at the heart of what constitutes the economy' (2006: 9), based on conflicting 'orders of generality' – that is, different systems for evaluating what matters, and different principles of order. Thus, forms of economic action based on personal ties and attachments are not simply archaic in the context of modern organizations, but rather indicate a distinct way of evaluating and bringing order to a situation, tied to a substantive philosophy (in this case one of loyalty). Thus, one cannot say that a particular way of organizing economic action is 'inappropriate', because the six 'orders of worth' that Boltanski and Thévenot initially outlined all represent possible moral principles for guiding action. A given actor in a given situation may draw upon these in justifying his or her behaviour to others, or in reaching some kind of compromise about how to proceed.

To claim that economic life involves multiple competing value systems is also to invoke a tradition, linked to Polanyi, which suggests that even under highly developed market systems, attempts to fully disembed economic actions from their social contexts are likely to fail, and indeed to lead to various kinds of 'counter-actions' (Polanyi 2001 [1944]). Thus, a variety of substantive values, including those antithetical to capitalism or markets, may co-exist alongside a dominant market or capitalist logic that many claim has wiped them out (see also Parry and Bloch 1989; Gibson-Graham 1996, 2006). From this perspective, looking at communication in contemporary economic life cannot simply mean analysing those symbolic forms that most clearly embody or propagate the market logics that dominate, but also those that criticize them or present alternatives.

This value plurality can be seen in what follows in various ways. On the one hand, the book uses mainly British and American examples. As such, it is describing market societies where most goods and services are exchanged via the market, but also capitalist societies where production is for profit, and wealth and productive assets are privately held. This affects the content and argument of the book in important ways. For example, chapters 3 and 4 detail many instances where capitalist profit motives decisively shape the communication environment and where debate is not about whether but about *how much* capitalism distorts communication or interferes with the availability of information. On the other hand, market societies do not only consist of market-based forms of exchange, and capitalist economies typically include – and even depend upon – non-capitalist institutions and alternative forms of transaction and provisioning (Gibson-Graham 1996, 2006; Slater and Tonkiss 2001). Thus, there are other economic logics and practices at work even in the heart of advanced capitalist systems. Some of these alternative logics and practices can be seen in the examples of online exchange and communication, and new forms of digital currency, discussed in chapter 4, while the fictional narratives discussed in chapter 5 give some sense of the alternative philosophies of economic life that circulate even within societies apparently dominated by the profit motive.

Taken together, the book suggests that the symbolic resources made available to us by media and communicative practices of various kinds do not only affirm some ascendant 'economistic' logic, capitalist or neoliberal; very often, they also provide the tools to resist or to challenge such frameworks. Just as the term 'economy' itself emerges differently in different sites and communicative practices, so the rules and norms governing acceptable and appropriate behaviour around money vary according to social context. While many societies, including the UK and US, have for some time been governed according to a logic that prioritizes markets and ideals of competitiveness, individual responsibility, entrepreneurialism and so forth, these societies also very often contain within them alternative traditions of thought, based on different values and moral systems. And these alternative ways of thinking about the economy tend to make themselves felt above all in the communicative and symbolic repertoires of those cultures. If we are to be optimistic about the possibility of economic change, it will be necessary to attend to these alternative ways of thinking.

Structure of the book

The book is divided into two parts. Part I considers the role of communication in economic life by exploring how economic actions, behaviours and practices can *themselves* be seen as communicative. In chapter 1, I explore how this idea has been developed in economic theory. Although economics seems to have little to say about communication, it actually has two quite distinctive perspectives. The first is the belief – seen in Adam Smith and much subsequent work – that economic actions are (non-verbal) forms of communication that can be observed as part of the market process. The second is the idea that 'communication' consists primarily in the acquisition or transfer of information. This idea has its roots in Hayek's work on price, and is then further developed in information economics and parts of game theory. The chapter traces the evolution of these views, before considering whether the discipline's approach to communication might be shifting in line with the rise of a more empirical trend in microeconomics.

Chapter 2 explores the same idea – that economic action is communicative – but through the lens of everyday practice. Treating communication as a form of symbolic interaction, it focuses on money, payments and price and shows that these have long functioned as 'media' for the communication of various feelings, affiliations and solidarities. This history is traced through strands of social scientific work, which help to explain why changes in these aspects of our economic lives are so consequential. In particular, monetary media hark back to the longstanding association between 'communication' and 'communion'; the changes associated with the decline of cash, the rise of alternative currencies or the emergence of dynamic pricing all revive longstanding tensions between money's power to generate collectivity ('communion') and its power to divide and exclude.

Part II shifts the focus of the book to explore how different types of discourse, and different communicative types, contribute to the structuring of economic life. In these chapters I adopt a broadly pragmatist approach to communication, focusing on the way that people or institutions attempt to 'do things with words' (Austin 1975). The forms of communication I consider – promotion, information, narrative and discussion – correspond loosely to different rhetorical modes or styles, although they are of course not exhaustive, and certainly not mutually exclusive.

Chapter 3 considers the role of promotion in shaping economic life. Promotion is typically associated with consumer culture and the matching of supply and demand, but the chapter shows that its role in our economic lives is much more wide-ranging. 'Promotional' communication is now a required element of many occupations other than retail (extending even to academics), and can be found in political speeches about the economy, central bank communications, and even economic theory. The chapter explores this extended scope of promotion, and shows, in the second half of the chapter, that the *media* of promotion are also often not quite what we think: contemporary promotion does not just flow through 'big' media and media institutions, but also through *materials* such as buildings, retail sites, credit cards and the behaviours and bodies of shop assistants. The chapter also considers the consequences of the fact that much promotional communication is either deliberately hidden or intended to sink into the unnoticed background of everyday life.

Chapter 4 addresses a quite different communicative practice: 'informing'. As a mode of discourse, informing is supposed to be open and uncoercive (Peters 1999). Similarly, the free flow of information – and its equal availability to all – is supposed to be central to the efficient functioning of markets as well as democracies (Schudson 2015). In this chapter I focus on the consequences of information abundance for online economies, and show that communication-as-information in fact constructs economic life in highly variable ways. On the one hand, both consumers and small businesses are advantaged by new types and volumes of information: it is easier to find information about goods and competitors; there are more opportunities for consumer 'voice' as well as 'exit'; private aspects of our economic lives can be discussed in ways that are often highly beneficial; and exchange can sometimes be 're-personalized' (Hart 2001). In many ways, information in our economic lives is a force for value plurality. At the same time, information is increasingly central to practices of concentration and control. Information about consumers is collected behind their backs automatically or semi-automatically, and is then sold and/or used to classify them in unknown but often highly consequential ways. 'Informing', in other words, is increasingly hidden from view and data is concentrated in the hands of a relatively small number of intermediaries who know how to interpret and deploy it. The chapter traces these developments before focusing in particular on the use of consumer information in digital marketing and online pricing.

In chapter 5 I examine the role of narratives and storytelling in economic life. I do this in two main ways: first, I look at literary and filmic treatments of economic life, and show that, historically, creative writers have often seen their role as opposing the values of the market. I then explore how these 'oppositional' values play out, and how certain recurrent economic concerns have become fuel for literary or filmic exploration. This includes an assessment of some of the problems that film, in particular, has had in representing capitalism and economic life. The chapter then turns to look at the economy itself as a narrated phenomenon, showing that, historically, the distinction between fact and fiction in written accounts of economic life was less clear and pronounced than it is now. The chapter explores both economists' and economic sociologists' interest in the role of narrative in constructing economic actions, and also examines the growing commercial uses of narrative – as in the case of 'brand storytelling' – to imbue companies and brands with meaning in the eyes of consumers and other stakeholders. Finally, the chapter considers the challenges to narrative forms of economic communication.

In chapter 6 I consider practices of discussion and deliberation – forms of communication that are often held to be superior to the one-way messages of media and culture (even the 'high culture' of literary narrative). Beginning with an analysis of economic discussion on television news and current affairs programmes, the chapter shows that these are often very far from the Habermasian ideal of rational-critical discourse. The tendency to simply put two opposing political viewpoints together with little commentary or explanation seems especially appealing in economic coverage, since it is an area that broadcasters often assume viewers find dull. Their response to this may be to attempt to create lively and engaging content through staged confrontations between political opponents. The chapter then considers the examples of audience discussion shows and online discussion forums. These do not meet ideals of deliberative debate either, but they do involve a wider range of people, and often construct economic life and economic concerns in ways that are dramatically different to television news. They also show that 'deliberation' is often combined with many other kinds of discourse. In the final part of the chapter, I look at some instances of 'everyday economics' that emerge in the less mediated spaces of daily life. These show – as I noted at the start of this introduction – that even a concept so apparently obvious as 'the economy' differs wildly in the way that it is understood in everyday contexts than in the mass media. Deliberation or debate about economic issues, here as elsewhere, is not a discrete type of discourse but deeply interwoven with other forms of communication. 'The economy', if it is understood at all, is understood in Weberian or Polanyian terms as the process of making ends meet, or alternatively as a power relation in which certain actors occupy a more advantageous position than others.

In the final chapter I revisit the book's main themes and propose some ways to develop the study of economic communication in the future. I re-evaluate the book's pragmatic approach to communication, assess what it leaves out, and explore how it might be taken up in more empirical contexts. I also spell out in more detail what a new framework for the study of communication and economic life might look like, and give concrete examples of areas that are often ignored by media and communications scholars but that would be fruitful avenues of enquiry. At the heart of any future research agenda there would be a focus on economic action as *meaningful*, rather than 'the economy' as powerful actors have already defined it. This does not mean abandoning critical scrutiny of those actors or of large institutions, but rather, by starting from what is meaningful in everyday life, attempting to connect public and political questions about economic communication to what C. Wright Mills called 'private troubles'. Doing this in turn allows us to think about the kinds of obligations that large and powerful institutions have to their audiences.

Part I

Economic action is communicative

This first part of the book, comprising two chapters, explores the communicative constitution of economic life by focusing on the ways economic actions and practices can *themselves* be seen as communicative. Chapter 1 considers how this idea has been advanced – mostly implicitly – in economic theory, while chapter 2 uses sociological and anthropological perspectives to draw attention to the symbolic communication associated with money, payment and price.

The two chapters provide contrasting accounts of communication in economic life, highlighting how different this term can look, depending on one's disciplinary perspective. Chapter 1 considers the way that market behaviours (typically, buying or not buying goods at particular price points) are construed as communicating information about consumers' preferences. It also looks at the way communication itself has been understood as quantities of information that can be acquired or transferred. Chapter 2 shows that the symbolism of monetary media (such as coins and tokens, but also prices) has historically allowed them to communicate various affiliations and solidarities, and how these are being remade in the light of changes to the infrastructure of payments. But these two chapters also differ quite markedly from what one might term 'mainstream' accounts of economic communication offered by media and communication studies. Instead of focusing on media coverage of established economic topics, they offer a way of thinking about economic communication as something much more ubiquitous, embedded both in the organization of economic infrastructures and activities, and in the day-to-day practices of ordinary citizens.

Chapter 1

Does *homo economicus* talk?
Communication in economic theory

In 1994, the US communications scholar James Carey claimed that after four decades, efforts to create a rapprochement between the disciplines of communications and economics must be deemed to have failed. It was clear, he said, that 'communications and economics constitute contradictory frameworks', and that they provide 'incommensurably alternative pictures of human action and social life'. Whereas economics is the theory and practice of allocating scarce resources, communication, he claimed, is 'the process of producing meaning, a resource that is anything but scarce'. As a result, the two disciplines inevitably 'confront one another blankly' and their only possible relation would be a countervailing one, in which communications 'establishes the challenge to the self-regarding preferences that undergird economic thinking'.

Carey laid the blame for this failure squarely at the door of economics, a discipline that, in its neoclassical formulation, could only engage with communication insofar as it could be reduced to a narrow, instrumental 'transmission' model. Like many human endeavours, communications had been 'so transformed by the theory and practice of economics that the former (communications as a practice, meaning as a resource) can hardly be recognized given the dominance of the latter' (1997 [1994]: 64). In this world of economics imperialism, any understanding of communication would be based on 'an evacuation of the resources of meaning in the service of profit and power'. Economics, in this view, can only conceive of communication as a commodity ('information') or an industry, and cannot accommodate its role as a qualitative, meaning-generating dimension of human behaviour or social life. The only option for the discipline of communications, in the face of this, would be to adopt a stance that emphasized the true, 'collective' spirit of communication whose work was the creation of a common and shared world.

Was Carey right to characterize economics in this way, and to draw these conclusions? His argument made it clear that he considered communications and economics to be 'historically' rather than 'ontologically' exclusive; he seemed to have in mind the possibility of a different understanding of economics based not simply on competition over scarce resources, but rather on something more akin to the substantivist notion of collective provisioning that I have sketched out in the introduction. What is less clear is whether Carey could also imagine an alternative account of communication. Any instance of communication as 'transmission ... for purposes of manipulation and control' seems, in Carey's slightly romanticized view, to be an aberration caused by the warping processes of late capitalism, rather than a possibility latent in all forms of human interaction.

This chapter does not seek to resolve Carey's question about the compatibility or otherwise of two disciplines. But it does share his view that communications scholars ought to be curious about how economists understand communication: if we are interested in the way communication shapes economic experience then we need to engage with the way economists think about communication. This matters because economic *theory* is often consequential for economic *practice*. As Donald MacKenzie and colleagues (2008) have shown, economic models are not simply abstract representations that stay in the academy, but often shape action in the real world. Economics can also shape how we think about the *meaningfulness* of economic events. It is the dominant social science, and the one most likely to be given the authority of a 'natural' science. Members of the civil service and government are more likely than ever before to have undergraduate degrees in economics or related subjects like business and accounting (Davis 2017: 598–9). News and other media also draw heavily on those with a background in economics – particularly economists from banks – in commenting on and contextualizing economic news. Thus, even if we know nothing about economics, our understanding of markets and of what we are doing when we participate in economic transactions is at least partly filtered through dominant narratives about what market exchange is and is not. This includes the extent to which it is a communicative, and therefore social, activity.

Economic theory seems at first glance to have little to say about communication. If hypothetical market actors are beings that discuss, argue, complain or persuade, such qualities remain mostly hidden in economic texts. The methodological individualism that underpins economic theory and modelling depends for its effectiveness on excluding those more complex interrelationships that make up much of social life. As Timothy Mitchell (2008) has observed, this is a problem if you think the task of economics is to represent an external world accurately, but much less so if you imagine its role is to organize markets or provide calculative tools and instruments. Indeed, most economists – as well as many other social scientists – would be happy to admit that their models are reductive, but would see the omission of complex ties as a worthwhile trade-off (e.g., Bénabou et al. 2018). My point in this chapter, however, is that a closer examination of economic texts reveals that, just like other social scientists, economists in fact *do* have implicit ideas about human nature and its typical forms of contact and association. Economic research and theorizing may be concerned with understanding how markets work, but in doing this it unavoidably also proposes implicit accounts of economic being together in the world, and thus of communication.

In the rest of the chapter I outline – in a necessarily selective way – some of what mainstream twentieth and early twenty-first-century economists have had to say (often implicitly rather than explicitly) about the interactional and informational basis of economic life. I focus on these mainstream approaches – rather than more critical or heterodox voices – because these are the ones that are most influential in business, government and the media, and which, rightly or wrongly, have come to speak for the discipline. Before this, however, I examine the idea – found in Adam Smith, but most developed in the notion of 'revealed preferences' – that economic action is *itself* a form of communication. This is in many ways the classic economic view (although as the next chapter shows, a version of it is shared by other disciplines). I then explore economists' understandings of the term 'information'. These, I think, are what Carey had in mind when he accused economists of reductionism. I outline key elements of contemporary information economics and show that while it places a substantive 'communicative' concept (i.e., information) at its heart, it remains within a broader tradition that sees communication in quantitative terms, and understands it as a series of discrete observable actions, rather than as dialogue or relationship. I briefly discuss the diversions from this found in some forms of game theory, before turning, in the final section, to some of the ways in which economics is changing. Drawing particularly on the growing empirical movement in the discipline, and on areas such as economic geography where the discipline has begun to have more contact with its neighbours, I show that some important work is being done that makes economics potentially more sensitive to the nature and consequences of human and mediated communication than it has been in the past.

Economic action is a form of communication

Perhaps the most obvious way in which economists bring communication and economic action together is in the principle – mostly implicit but occasionally explicit – that economic action is *itself* a form of communication. This idea has been expressed most fluently in Albert Hirschman's (1970) *Exit, Voice, and Loyalty*, but its antecedents can be found in Adam Smith's observations about the parallels between trading and conversation, as well as in the concept of revealed preferences developed by Paul Samuelson and others. References to the parallels between linguistic interaction and market exchange can be found across Smith's work. In *The Wealth of Nations* (1991 [1776]), he posits a causal connection between a primary urge to trade and exchange and forms of human contact and sociability centred on the marketplace. The recognition of interdependence that results from this contact – the sense that my self-interest depends upon some degree of contact and cooperation with you – is what drives social harmony and solidarity. The 'exchanges' that occur in the marketplace are inevitably not only of goods, but also of words and information, but these latter are presumed to have been driven in the first instance by self-interest. Given this, the account of communication offered here is limited to the transmission of information; whatever happens in practice in market encounters, in theoretical terms it remains at the level of what Peters (1999: 6) describes as 'the successful linkage of two separate termini'. In Smith's earlier *Theory of Moral Sentiments* (first published in 1759), by contrast, a wider canvas is drawn, and human motivation is theorized not only in terms of the seeking out of others for self-interested purposes, but also in terms of the desire for 'mutual sympathy of sentiments'. Indeed, the desire for mutual sympathy is considered by Smith to be one of the two basic motivations in life (Otteson 2002: 5). The capacity to 'imaginatively change places' with others, to understand the world from their point of view, and to seek this out *as an end in itself* points towards a more profound understanding of communication, involving greater reciprocity, fellow feeling and a sense of 'contact between interiorities' (Peters 1999: 6–7).

Which of these is the 'real' Smith? The 'Adam Smith problem' (Tribe 2008) has often been settled by assuming that the desire to better our position is what drives our economic actions, while the desire for mutual sympathy motivates all the other, presumably non-economic, actions. And yet the history and anthropology of markets suggests that things are not so clear: people routinely blend their economic and their intimate encounters

(Zelizer 2005) and markets are key sites of social and civic interaction. It is not always clear where our economic actions end and our non-economic actions begin. Indeed, the *doux commerce* thesis (the idea that commerce softens and refines otherwise 'barbarian' passions) with which Smith and others were associated comes from an earlier non-commercial meaning of the term 'commerce': 'besides trade, the word long denoted animated and repeated conversation and other forms of polite social intercourse and dealings among persons (frequently between two persons of the opposite sex)' (Hirschman 1977: 61). In this account, the development of commerce involves extending a pre-existing communicative world motivated by non-economic concerns into new realms. In fact, the order of precedence between the urge to trade and the urge to communicate is hard to untangle. David Graeber suggests that for Smith, 'logic and conversation are really just forms of trading' (2011: 25), and thus that trade is the original form of, and reason for, contact and communication. And yet in the *Lectures on Jurisprudence* from which this claim is taken, Smith also talks of the 'natural inclination every one has to persuade' (offering a shilling is really 'offering an argument') (2011: 394). From this perspective, it is equally plausible to argue that trade is really just a form of conversation or a socially elaborated version of the impulse to persuade.

Interestingly, there is some evidence that Smith's idea that markets are sites of spontaneous order itself derives from his earlier work on language. Smith's short essay 'Considerations concerning the first formation of languages', although published after *The Theory of Moral Sentiments*, was written earlier and contains within it a model of human interaction that would inform his whole oeuvre. In this account, linguistic development occurs not as the result of any top-down instruction or central command, but rather on the basis of 'on-the-spot trial and error, without any antecedent, overall plan' (Otteson 2002: 278). The 'desire to communicate some specific new need' drives language development (p. 266), and it is through usage – 'a continuous, free exchange of words' – that rules emerge, rather than vice versa. The implications of this for later ideas about the spontaneous order of markets are clear, and it is Otteson's claim that the germ of Smith's key ideas about market order and the 'invisible hand' were first developed in his speculations on language.

The export of these naturalistic ideas about communication and language into a model of market exchange as both benign and self-regulating raises some interesting questions. To the extent that classical political economy was concerned with questions of social and political order, it is perhaps unsurprising that its key theorist would turn to ideas about language and communication that saw it as a force for social integration and solidarity rather than as a site of manipulation or antagonism. And yet, as Hirschman points out, the connotations of gentility and politeness that the non-commercial history of the term 'commerce' brought with them seemed very strange in an era when the slave trade was at its peak (1977: 62). But it is not just the nature of trade that is treated partially in this analogy; it is also the nature of communication. Both the idea of commerce as animated but polite conversation, or the idea that languages, like markets, develop relatively smoothly into a series of conventional rules and customs, underplay the extent to which linguistic communication is itself fraught with power play and manipulation. The evolution of language is by no means something that emerges entirely 'naturally' or consensually or with no negative sanctions.[1] This does not necessarily mean that Smith was wrong about language, but it does show that these characterizations of communication are highly partial, and that definitions of communication – as models of how humans can be together in the world – in turn have consequences for the models of economic action with which they become associated.

A second example of the way economists have treated economic actions as forms of communication is through the concept of revealed preferences. Associated with Paul Samuelson and Lionel Robbins, the idea emerged from attempts to model consumer behaviour and choice in ways that could be based on observation alone. This in turn was an attempt to avoid the concept of 'utility', which seemed to depend – uncomfortably for many economists – on psychological or philosophical underpinnings (Wong 1978). Thus, according to the logic of revealed preferences, if a consumer buys bundle of goods x (say, two apples and three bananas) rather than bundle of goods y (say, one banana and four apples) that are of equivalent price, then the former bundle is 'revealed preferred'. From this, one can reconstruct their preferences for use in a variety of situations (see also Hargreaves Heap and Varoufakis 1995).

My interest here is not with the value of the term within economics[2] but rather with what the concept reveals about understandings of communication. To state the rather obvious, Samuelson's theory assumes that the best way to learn about people's preferences is by observing their behaviour, rather than by talking to them. Yet as Amartya Sen has pointed out, this would make much more sense if economists were studying animals. Indeed, Sen highlights revealed preferences as a key example of the problems for economics of relying on 'distanced' forms of knowing, akin to those of the natural sciences, when studying beings for whom choice is 'in a fundamental sense, always a social act' (1973: 253). Quite apart from the problems of assuming that choices reflect preferences, that preferences remain fixed or constant, or that any such preferences are consciously and rationally formed, Sen argues that 'the thrust of the revealed preference approach has been to undermine ... *talking* as a method of knowing about others' (1973: 258, emphasis added). Economics, he suggests, has tended to overstate the problems associated with methods involving direct communication, while underestimating those based on observation.

The idea that economic actors are to be understood through what they *do* rather than what they *say* is deeply rooted in both economics and those parts of psychology that have influenced it. Hirschman (1970) captures this most effectively in his analysis of the difference between 'exit' and 'voice'. When people express their dissatisfaction with an organization by leaving it, or no longer buying its products, this is known as 'exit'; by contrast, if they express their dissatisfaction directly through complaining or protesting, this is known as 'voice' (1970: 2–4). For Hirschman, while the latter belongs to the realm of politics, exit 'belongs to the realm of economics' and is 'the sort of mechanism economics thrives on':

> It is neat – one either exits or one does not; it is impersonal – any face-to-face confrontation between customer and firm with its imponderable and unpredictable elements is avoided and success and failure of the organization are communicated to it by a set of statistics; and it is indirect – any recovery on the part of the declining firm comes by courtesy of the Invisible Hand, as an unintended by-product of the customer's decision to shift. (1970: 15–16)

Hirschman goes on to note that whereas economists would see the 'voice' option as messy, cumbrous and inefficient, and 'exit' as far more direct, 'a person less well trained in economics might naively suggest that the direct way of expressing views is to express them!' (1970: 17).

This gets to the heart of what we might call a distinctively 'economic' approach to communication (at least in neoclassical choice theory): it is non-dialogical. Expression takes place through actions rather than words, and interpretation occurs by drawing inferences from the observation of actions at a distance, rather than through conversations in which utterances are clarified in an ongoing fashion. Of course, the idea that 'actions speak louder than words' is pervasive in many spheres beyond economics, and economists are not the only ones who suspect that 'direct' communication between humans may confuse as much as it explains. But this model of communication as a fundamentally non-sensuous form of contact (Peters 1999), to do with signals rather than speech, is vitally important in distinguishing economic knowledge of the world. To know other people through entirely disembodied forms of contact is also, as Katherine Hayles (1999) observes, a crucial part of the transition from 'communication' to 'information'.

Communication is information plus signalling

The concept of information, with associated notions such as screening and signalling, is now perhaps the dominant way in which economists think about communication. The 'turn to information' has been a significant and enduring one, and is at the core of Carey's criticism – noted at the beginning of the chapter – that economists can only think about communication in quantitative, measurable terms. But is his criticism fair? To assess the meaning of economics' reliance on the concept of information, it is necessary to trace a little of how it has evolved.

The roots of information thinking in economics are usually traced to the 1930s and the shift of focus away from market *equilibrium* and towards dynamic market *processes* (Slater and Tonkiss 2001: 52; Mirowski 2002). In a key essay, Hayek (1945) foregrounds the role of price – explicitly characterized as an information signal – as both an input into and outcome of market action. He claims that the information on which people base their plans, and the way that this is communicated to others, is *'the crucial problem'* for economic theory (p. 520, emphasis added). This 'problem' does not require the help of a central authority, but can be solved by the price system. This is because the price system is *itself* 'a mechanism for communicating information', and far more efficient than any centralized authority could ever be. He goes on:

> ... in abbreviated form, [and] by a kind of symbol, only the most essential information is passed on, and passed on only to those concerned. It is more than a metaphor to describe the price system as a kind of machinery for registering change, or a system of telecommunications which enables individual producers to watch merely the movement of a few pointers ... in order to adjust their activities. (Hayek 1945: 527)

Hayek's work is an important precursor to information economics, so it is worth exploring his understanding of communication in more detail. First, questions of knowledge and information are primarily quantitative: for Hayek the only thing a hypothetical market actor needs to know is *'how much more or less* difficult to procure certain things have become ...

or how much more or less urgently wanted are the alternative things he produces or uses' (p. 525, emphasis in original). All information can be contained within the existing 'economic calculus', and worlds are disclosed through numbers not words. This is what allows economic information to be understood through a parallel with telecommunications. Secondly, communication is mechanical: price information is transmitted through a 'mechanism', a 'kind of machinery', or a 'system of telecommunications', and the receivers of this information 'watch merely the movement of a few pointers, as an engineer might watch the hands of a few dials, in order to adjust their activities to changes of which they may never know more than is reflected in the price movement' (1945: 527).

This characterization of the market as a system of telecommunication, and communication as a semi-automatic process, anticipated developments in computation and cybernetics research that would occur at the RAND Corporation during and after the Second World War (Mirowski 2002). There, the effort to turn information from a general into a scientific concept – one that could bridge the worlds of mathematics, engineering and computing – meant that the term lost many of its older and more flexible connotations (Gleick 2011: 7–8). The most obvious one was any conception of information as embodied. Hayles (1999), for example, traces the process by which information was construed as a disembodied entity that can flow between other entities, separate from the specific material forms and contexts in which it is embedded, and which is free to travel across time and space. In Shannon and Wiener's work, information has clearly been separated from any sense of meaning, and thus can be treated as stable across contexts (1999: 53).

The other notable effect of this work on information and computation has to do with the military connotations of the link between 'information' and its forerunner 'intelligence'. When Shannon described his work in 1939, he said that he was working on 'the fundamental properties of general systems for the transmission of *intelligence*' (cited in Gleick 2011: 7, emphasis added), and in the US as elsewhere, interest in information theory was heavily influenced by military concerns (Yoshimi 2006). As Mirowski (2002: 17) notes, this military inspiration for cybernetic research extended beyond mere everyday logistics and funding – it often 'imposed an imperative of "command, control, communications, and information"' upon the questions asked and the solutions proposed. For Mirowski, this logic finds its highest point in the Cold War 'rationality of the paranoid' of John Nash's game theory. Yet as the term 'information' becomes ubiquitous and takes on an air of neutrality, its associations with (military) intelligence become obscured, and its connotations of control over others through knowledge, intelligence or strategy sink back into the background.

The entry of information into the mainstream of economic thinking is typically traced to the 1970s: to a paper by Akerlof (1970) on the second-hand car market, or to work examining the effect of 'expectations' about macroeconomic variables (Fine and Milonakis 2009). In contrast to Hayek, for whom all necessary information was contained in price, the concept of information emerging from the work of Akerlof, Stiglitz, Spence and others is more plural, if only in the sense that there are many kinds of information, other than price, that actors might need for markets to function efficiently (Slater and Tonkiss 2001). In Akerlof's account, the information that consumers need in order to buy a car is whether the car is good or bad quality – something that may itself be composed of various 'informational' elements, such as frequency of accidents, repairs and so on. In the case of used cars, the seller has this information but the buyer does not, and price is not a good guide. In fact, the information asymmetry regarding quality will push prices down, because most buyers will only be willing to pay the price of an 'average' quality car. This in turn will lead to the exit of high-quality sellers (those who own 'peaches'), which will lower average prices even further, until only 'lemons' (i.e., low-quality cars) are left. In the case of work on expectations, an initial interest in expectations about macroeconomic variables such as inflation gradually leads to 'a focus more generally upon information availability' across many variables, and then, more specifically, to the 'micro-information available to individual agents undertaking transactions with each other' (Fine and Milonakis 2009: 59).

Much of information economics deals with the consequences of *asymmetric* information, rather than with the nature of information itself. However, the field's key concepts almost always reiterate an earlier logic of communication as action rather than interaction. To take some examples, 'adverse selection' (the fact that risky customers may be more likely to buy certain kinds of products, such as insurance) and 'moral hazard' (the fact that, once a certain product is purchased, people have less incentive to behave carefully) both refer to the real-world consequences of imperfect, asymmetric information, and have little say about how communication figures more positively in exchange. And yet even the more 'pro-active' concepts in information theory – those that refer to forms of communicative activity taken to offset problems – maintain a view of communication as primarily an *observable action* rather than any kind of sustained interaction or dialogue. Thus 'screening' (introducing techniques to make people reveal more information about themselves, usually for the purposes of classification or pricing) and 'signalling' (pro-actively providing information in order to help buyers make decisions) are both cases where communication takes the form of action, rather than speech (see also Hirschman 1970). Signals, for Spence, are *things one does* that are visible and that are in part designed to communicate' (2002: 434, emphasis added), while screening is about 'confront[ing] people with schedules that cause them to make appropriate choices [and] in so doing to reveal themselves' (p. 435). This is consistent with an economic worldview in which 'actions speak louder than words', as I have outlined above. Information does indeed appear in this work as something that is either present or absent, complete or incomplete, and that may perhaps be thought of as a form of 'intelligence' for human transactions.

In the case of both signalling and screening, communicative actions are assumed to be costly to agents, and engaging in them thus involves calculating net benefits. Yet while the concept of signalling has gained a wide purchase, the characterization of signalling as a costly action is being confronted with an empirical reality in which 'voice' (to use Hirschman's terms) is no longer more costly than 'exit' in all situations. If we think, for example, about the sheer volume of customer feedback generated by e-commerce sites and social media platforms, and the work that goes into sorting them, it becomes clear that market actors, even if not economists, are already having to think about the messy gradations of 'voice' that range from purely quantitative purchasing data to one-to-one correspondence with individual consumers.

Communication is the strategic use of information: game theory

The claim I have been making so far – that information economics continues to treat communication as a series of discrete actions that can be externally observed and that provide information, rather than as *inter*actions between parties engaged in ongoing relationships – is slightly more complicated in the field of game theory, whose origins precede information economics, but which is arguably more complex in its view of communication. The possession or absence of information is still a core concern, but unlike standard decision theory, which does not involve taking other actors' choices into account, game theory is concerned with actors 'who are conscious that their actions affect each other' (Rasmusen 2001 [1989]: 11). With its consequent focus on strategy, conflict and cooperation, game theory has a more distinctive perspective on what economic communication looks like. Although possession of information is still central, the construct of 'the game' makes use of understandings of human association and communication that are otherwise rarely present in most classical or neoclassical work.

Consider first of all the distinction between cooperative and non-cooperative games. Early proponent of game theory John von Neumann spent much of *Theory of Games and Economic Behavior* talking about 'coalitions', among which he includes trade unions, consumers' cooperatives and industrial cartels (1953: 15). His discussion of the 'state of information' in various games like chess or poker is explicitly linked to questions of communication (or its impossibility) between players, and whether they are in alliances or simply opposition. While chess is a (conflictual) game of strategy with perfect information, in which all players know all previous moves, the less perfect, more typical games have outcomes that depend on chance or uncertainty too. In those games, the ability to communicate or avoid communicating is key. In bridge, for example, the fact that two players are on the same 'side', and must cooperate with each other but are forbidden from cooperating with other players, means that communication – 'i.e. the exchange of information' (von Neumann and Morgenstern 1953: 53) – is restricted. This gives rise to 'a very well known component of practical strategy ... the possibility of signaling'. In this context, 'the interest of the player ... lies in promoting the "signaling", i.e. the spreading of information, within his own organization', and this, in turn, gives rise to 'the elaborate system of "conventional signals" in Bridge', which are 'parts of the strategy, and not rules of the game' (von Neumann and Morgenstern 1953: 53–4). In poker, the interest of the player lies in preventing signalling, something that is achieved through 'irregular and seemingly illogical behavior' (i.e., bluffing) designed to 'make it harder for the opponent to draw inferences' and which 'makes the "signal" uncertain and ambiguous' (p. 54).

The modelling of games as either cooperative or non-cooperative has implications for communication. The cooperative element of some games (like bridge) leads to conventional, shared forms of communication; the non-cooperative, or conflictual, element of games like poker may lead to forms of communication that are deliberately misleading, deceitful or are calculated to produce uncertainty. Both accounts of communication represent a step away from the 'animated conversation' and 'polite social intercourse' of classical political economy, and a more complex view of human interaction than later information theoretic approaches, which are often concerned simply with information's presence or absence. But conflict and cooperation also have different implications for communication in the deeper sense of what Peters (1999) calls 'contact between interiorities'. As Schelling puts it:

> In the pure-coordination game, the player's objective is to *make contact with the other player through some imaginative process of introspection*, of searching for shared clues; in the minimax strategy of a zero-sum game … one's whole objective is to avoid any meeting of minds, even an inadvertent one. (Schelling 1960: 96, emphasis added)

In Mirowski's account of information economics and game theory, he is very critical of the 'rationality of the paranoid' that he attributes, in particular, to John Nash's work. It demands, he suggests, the 'total reconstruction of the thought process of the Other – *without* communication, *without* interaction, *without* cooperation' (2002: 343–4, emphasis in original). This is no doubt true, but in the work of writers like Schelling, where cooperation or coordination are practical components of many game situations, communication comes a lot closer to something that communications theorists themselves would recognize. In Stephen Levinson's (2006) linguistic account of interaction, for example, Schelling's 'shared mirror world' (the ability to simulate the other's simulation of oneself, and to imaginatively change places with them) is at the basis of a whole pragmatic order. It is the human capacity to reflexively imagine how the other might think of them, and then to check or test these assumptions in an ongoing way, that makes coordination and cooperation possible.

One final point, related to this, is that dynamic or repeated games (or games where there are multiple 'rounds') also have implications for communication and for the social relationships it expresses and nurtures. The repetition of a game – in practice, repeated exchanges between 'players' – expands the range of strategic and communicative options available. There is the possibility of punishing or rewarding other players for the ways they have played in the past, for learning about others' typical strategies, and for players to gain – and exploit – reputations for behaving in a certain way (Hargreaves Heap and Varoufakis 1995). There is also the possibility of greater cooperation in repeated versions of the game, especially when there is no knowledge of when a game will end. The explicit forms of communication at work here – observing others' actions as a form of communication – are not so different from other areas of economic thought, but the sense of sustained contact between interiorities is much greater.

The concept of information at the heart of information theory remains very reductive: it refers to 'knowable stochastic information, effectively data' (Fine and Milonakis 2009: 60) and is understood as 'something agents have or do not have and play no part in creating other than through their actions or signals'. Outside of the discipline of economics, the role of information and knowledge in market processes has been expanded in ways that suggest direct human interaction and communication are important too: Preda (2009), for example, argues that social relationships such as 'gossip at the water fountain' can provide valuable information, while Velthuis (2005) has described the intricate relationship between stories and narratives told by art dealers and the prices of the artworks they sell. In any case, the broader point is that information and knowledge gleaned from other humans, however indirectly, are now treated as a source of market efficiency and therefore as something to include within economic theory.

Recent developments: a new role for communication?

So far I have outlined what I take to be the most persistent, general conceptualization of communication within economic theory (i.e., the idea that economic action is itself a form of communication, and more 'efficient' than other forms) and the most significant characterization of communication by twentieth-century economists, namely the concept of information. The development of information economics, in particular, seems to confirm the prejudice of communications scholars, that economists can only imagine communication in ways that are both quantifiable and priceable. On the other hand, it is worth noting that the idea that economic action is *itself* communicative or symbolic is something that economics shares with other social scientific disciplines, such as anthropology and sociology. It is also important to note that the field of economics has itself been changing. Over the past forty years the discipline has become more empirically focused, with many more publications that are empirical in content than in the past, and empirical papers being more highly cited (Angrist et al. 2017; Montesinos and Brice 2019). This means that some assumptions about communication implicit in earlier models are being subtly challenged and reworked. In this final section of the chapter, I want to highlight three ways in which different sub-fields of economics are expanding their conceptions of communication. The first two are from empirical microeconomics. The third is from the field of finance, where the perceived failures of existing models have led some economists to speculate in a more wide-ranging way about the role of communication in market processes.

The first area I want to consider is urban economics and economic geography. In the same way that game theorists developed a more explicit account of communication because they recognized that not all decisions could be modelled at the level of an individual, so too in urban economics has the fact of human communication and contact become a necessary part of the conceptual framework. Focused as it is on questions of *where* economic activity takes place, and why that should be so, urban and spatial economics has long been concerned with the particular attractiveness of cities, and other sites of human agglomeration, for companies and workers. In addition to their communications and transport infrastructures, one advantage of cities, from an economic perspective, is that the dense populations offer opportunities to learn from others, and thus for innovation to happen. This learning activity, as Duranton and Puga (2003: 36) observe, is typically 'not a solitary activity taking place in a void [but] involves interactions with others and many of these interactions have a "face-to-face" nature'. Although modelling such interactions and their economic effects may require economists to describe communications quantitatively (e.g., interactions must involve the transfer of quantities of information, the experience of a particular duration, or measurable outputs such as patents), and this in turn means that 'communication' is understood quite conventionally (as transmission, imitation, etc.), it is still accorded a centrality to human action that is not so true of other parts of the discipline.

More interesting, perhaps, is the fact that since urban and spatial economists are interested in how and when place comes to matter to economic activity, they have also become interested in the consequences of *mediated* communication for economic life; that is, whether ubiquitous connectivity and the hypothetical ability to work from anywhere renders agglomeration benefits redundant (e.g., Grabher and Ibert 2014). While some authors have developed models of the specific and continuing value of face-to-face communication for particular sectors of the economy (e.g., Storper and Venables 2004), others are beginning to explore what mediated communication tools can add to the knowledge creation and learning processes. Thus Grabher and Ibert (2014) argue not only that 'hybrid online communities' can compensate for the lack of sensory clues associated with 'being there', but also that there are specific affordances associated with virtual or mediated collaboration that are 'unattainable in face-to-face only settings' (2014: 100). These include features like quasi-anonymity, which can lead to a 'redistribution of influence from formal status to competence', with the more efficient circulation of credible information the result. Similarly, the long-duration and archiving of online discussions make knowledge available for review and revisiting in ways that are barely ever true of face-to-face meetings (pp. 114–16).

As remote working becomes more common, it is possible that scholars in this field will be led to draw upon concepts from media and communications proper, where researchers have already identified a number of principles governing the way actors select among different communicative options according to task or register (see, e.g., Madianou and Miller 2013). This suggests that while the overall logic of economic thought may continue to prioritize understandings of communication as information search and transfer, this is not necessarily true in applied areas, where varieties of communication may in fact emerge as part of the answer to particular empirical questions.

This kind of development is reflected in a second example, from studies of the management of common pool resources. In one such case, Elinor Ostrom (1990) tests and challenges assumptions derived from game theory about the logic of collective action. Specifically, she shows that conceiving of common pool resource management (e.g., the management of fishing rights) as an essentially non-cooperative prisoners' dilemma game can lead to inappropriately sweeping conclusions about people's ability to cooperate that do not accurately reflect real-world behaviour. What is more, to the extent that these conclusions influence policy, they may have further ramifications in making problems harder to solve. Thus, while economic theory – in the form of a game-theoretic version of the 'tragedy of the commons' – would see cooperation in the use of common resources as unlikely, Ostrom's empirical work finds something different. She is able to show that there are a number of factors influencing the likely success of attempts to solve common pool resource management problems. One of these is communication; in failed attempts to escape prisoner's dilemma-type scenarios, 'the participants may simply have *no capacity to communicate* with one another, no way to develop trust, and no sense that they must share a common future' (1990: 21, emphasis added). By contrast, when participants are able to communicate and build up trust, they can make binding contracts 'to commit themselves to a cooperative strategy that they themselves will work out' (1990: 15). Very simply, then, Ostrom uses empirical work to show that the principle of non-cooperation – of individuals with inevitably opposing interests – may sometimes be wrong.

In a final example, various writers have attempted to explain how cultural and communicative factors may shape financial markets. One currently fashionable area of research concerns the role of narrative (e.g., Akerlof and Shiller 2009; Bénabou et al. 2018), something I will explore a little further in chapter 5. But there has also been an interest in the mediating role of technologies. Robert Shiller, for example, shares with various economists an interest in the performative or perlocutionary powers of language – for example, the use of careful language by central bank chairs to 'talk up' or 'talk down' the market (2005). But Shiller adds to this an interest in the role of communications technology in extending or amplifying what Keynes called animal spirits and Alan Greenspan termed 'irrational exuberance'. In describing how speculative bubbles and crashes occur, he notes that while there may be a series of structural precipitating factors – supportive monetary policy, an expansion in media reporting of business news, the rise of day traders and so on – these are all 'amplified' in various ways, such that the impact of the initial increases in a stock's price leads to 'much larger price increases than the factors themselves would have suggested' (2005: 68–9).

Shiller's technological language of amplification mechanisms and feedback loops is only partly metaphorical, since one of the 'mechanisms' that interests him is the news media. Media, he suggests, are:

> fundamental propagators of speculative price movements through their efforts to make news interesting to their audience. They sometimes strive to enhance such interest by attaching news stories to stock market movements that the public has already observed, thereby enhancing the salience of these movements and focusing greater attention on them. (2005: 95)

Shiller's interest in news media is partly as propagators of narratives and stories (see also Akerlof and Shiller 2009) and partly as technologies that enhance salience through repetition and wide-scale distribution. He is also interested – as many finance scholars are – in the psychology of crowd behaviour (see Borch and Lange 2017 for a discussion), but for Shiller there is an important communicative dimension to this, which others often miss. Specifically, he discerns a link between imitative herd behaviour and the spread of electronic media. For him, the 'explosion of techno-logical innovation' that facilitates communication has consequences for markets because it 'may have the effect of expanding ... the interpersonal contagion of ideas' (2005: 182). It may do this in part because electroni-cally mediated information often lacks the elements of 'another person's voice, another person's facial expressions, another person's emotions' that might be associated with trust and cooperation. By contrast, Shiller places much store by the power of face-to-face communication – and in particular collective discussion and deliberation – to help people avoid engaging in imitative behaviour that may be individually rational but is collectively irrational and leads to bad outcomes. For all his interest in technology, in other words, Shiller's solution to the pathologies of finance is a curiously old-fashioned version of communication.

Although the mainstream of economic thinking continues to conceptualize communication in terms of actions and inferences about actions, or as discrete chunks of information, rather than as a process of discussion or mediated dialogue, these examples suggest that the situation may be beginning to change. In some areas, such as urban economics, communication and contact between people are evidently central to the phenomena being explained, and thus must be acknowledged conceptually. In others, such as Ostrom's work, communication is an empirical finding that helps to explain deviations from an assumed non-cooperative state, and thus outcomes that are better than game-theoretic models would predict. In Shiller's work, dropping the presumption of rationality creates space to posit forms of communication based not on observation of action or the acquisition of information, but rather on 'contagion' and emotional impulses. At the same time, the highly mediated nature of market information can no longer be ignored and requires Shiller to consider how mass media extend, amplify or even distort what were once considered to be relatively unambiguous market 'signals'. To counteract the negative outcomes associated with this, Shiller interestingly turns not to the individual pursuit of information but to the 'interpersonal face-to-face and word-of-mouth communication that developed over millions of years' (2005: 180), and to the capacities of people to 'pool their first impressions and discuss these as a group' (2005: 178).

Conclusion

If we are interested in the way that communication constructs economic experience – including our understanding of the term 'economy' itself – then it is vital to look at the implicit and explicit characterizations of communication offered in economic theory. Economists' models of the world, like other social scientific theories, contain implicit accounts of human nature and ways of being together in the world. Thus, economists' ideas about communication – including whether they have one at all – are important measures of their understanding of human relatedness. With this in mind, the chapter began with a question: are communications scholars right to characterize economists' views of communication as being concerned only with the quantitative and measurable concept of 'information'? Is the economic view of human communication so reductive that there can be no meaningful dialogue between the two traditions? As I hope has become clear, there are indeed important respects in which Carey was right in his characterization. The information theory from which economics draws so heavily was, as John Durham Peters (1999) reminds us, always intended to be a theory of 'signals not significance', and in many aspects of economic research it is true that the concept of information is useful only to the extent that it is quantifiable.

However, there are also some important qualifications to this answer. The first is that while the characterization is fair for the discipline as a whole, communication may be treated quite differently in particular sub-fields. There are, for example, areas such as those examined by Ostrom, where empirical work has challenged dominant theoretical models that assume the impossibility of collaboration. In other areas, such as urban economics and, increasingly, aspects of macroeconomics, economists might well try to quantify the *outputs* and significance of communications for the areas of economic activity in which they are interested, but their underlying understanding of what communication might entail is often more wide-ranging and subtle than Carey's position allows. It should also be noted that in many areas of empirical microeconomics, written communication of various kinds are increasingly becoming a *source* of data, as in the use of corpus linguistic methods and tools. This too suggests that the communicative aspects of economic activity are becoming more relevant to the economic outputs and consequences in which economists are most interested. Taken together, developments in the discipline (which is becoming more empirical), its methods, as well as its objects of study (which are becoming more complex) are making the characterization of economists as only interested in the narrowest visions of communication less and less accurate.

The second important qualification is that Carey's understanding of the discipline ignores what is perhaps the most overarching, if implicit, 'economic' view of communication, which is that economic actions are *themselves* forms of communication. Media and communications scholars do not often consider this 'symbolic' aspect of economic action in any depth, since their interests more typically focus on mediated interaction and dialogue. By contrast, and as we shall see in the next chapter, sociologists and anthropologists have shown more interest in the ways in which economic action can be communicative, even if their motivations and interests in studying it are somewhat different to those of economists. In fact, the question of what and how economic actions communicate is of growing practical importance, as companies try to mine customers' behavioural data for clues about their tastes, preferences and ability to pay. Indeed, the sense in which we communicate information about our economic lives – and others communicate with us – even in the absence of verbal or written expression, is now at the heart of many important political and economic debates. It is to these symbolic forms of economic communication that I therefore now want to turn.

Chapter 2

The symbolism of money, payment and price

In the previous chapter I looked at the way communication figures in economists' models of the world. I showed that many economists see observable actions, rather than interactions, as the most reliable forms of communication from which preferences or other valuable information can be deduced. In this chapter, I consider a range of other ways in which economic actions can be seen as communicative. In particular, I focus on the symbolic dimensions of economic life, with a special focus on the symbolism of money, payment and price. Money symbolism is one of the most common ways in which economic action can be said to be communicative, and yet studies of such symbolic communication are more common in the disciplines of sociology, anthropology and psychoanalysis than in media and communications itself.

At the heart of symbolism is the capacity of one thing to stand in for another: on UK coins and banknotes, for example, the head of Queen Elizabeth can 'stand in' metonymically for the authority of the state. But this symbolism can work at other levels too. From a child's point of view, a parental gift of book vouchers rather than cash might equally 'stand in' for – i.e., symbolize or represent – attempts to control them or restrict their choices. Money lends itself to this kind of symbolic elaboration precisely *because* it is so widely understood as a neutral medium that refers only to pure quantity (Simmel 1978; O'Malley 2011). It is, in Martijn Konings's terms, money's 'mundane futility, its emphatic nothingness' that makes it a source of 'practically infinite demands and so central a point of orientation for earthly activity' (2015: 6). The ways in which different actors give colour and meaning to this apparently 'empty' medium – whether through official decree, informal norms and customs, or purely private meanings – is at the heart of money's capacity to communicate symbolically.

Part of what makes money so powerful, then, is that it not only shapes our material wellbeing, but is also able to stand in for – and thus communicate – other less tangible aspects of how we feel, including our sense of identity and connection to other people. As I will show, money and payment, but sometimes even the price we pay for goods, have long been media for communicating meaning, and for binding social groups together. This is especially clear in the case of national currencies, and payments made by the state, but it can also be traced in things like shared knowledge of the price of goods. These shared or collective relationships to money are why changes to monetary systems – in the form of alternative currencies, new payment systems and 'personalized' pricing that I describe in the second half of the chapter – are potentially such significant shifts. Technologies that give individual consumers greater autonomy may also threaten to isolate them, and technologies that allow smaller groups to act collectively in their own interest may also allow them to generate new forms of exclusion and division. Towards the end of the chapter I will show that these changes to the organization of money, payment and price dramatize a longstanding tension between money's power to bind together (i.e., communication as community) and its power to divide, and between its status as a resource for meaning-making or as a means of exclusion.

Money's symbolic qualities

Money's symbolism has been observed by a range of authors, some working in a more philosophical register, which looks at the symbolic aspects of exchange in general, while others take a more sociological approach to the symbolism of particular monetary tokens such as coins, notes, cards and, more recently, electronic or digital payments. Jean-Joseph Goux's analysis of 'symbolic economies' suggests logical parallels between the function of language and the function of money, and then extends this to other systems in which 'the play of substitutions defines qualitative values' (1990: 3). In Goux's view, it is not so much that money is 'like' language or that language is 'like' economic exchange, but rather that both systems operate through the 'radical operation of substitution', i.e., that aspect of symbolism in which one thing 'stands in for' or 'takes the place of' another. This operation is radical because for one thing to stand in for, or stand in place of, another thing is to imply 'equivalence despite difference' – 'the maintenance of an ideality through changes in materiality' (p. 2). For Goux, in structuralist mode, 'the connection between signifier and signified [in language] is as fragile, random, and arbitrary as the one that endows a piece of base metal or a rectangle of paper with market value' (1990: 102). Equally, Goux argues that, in almost all symbolic systems, one signifier becomes elevated above the others, and is used as a standard or benchmark against which they can be measured.

Goux's philosophical take on money as a symbolic system can be contrasted with more empirical and historical approaches, which focus on the symbolism of monetary tokens rather than the money system. Michael Billig (1995) includes national currencies as one of the media of 'banal nationalism' – all of the small ways in which the nation is flagged in everyday life and through which we are encouraged to think of the nation as a natural unit with which to identify. Monetary tokens can symbolize the authority of the nation itself – to set up one's own currency is to signal one's intentions towards statehood, as in the case of militant Islamist group ISIS, which, in 2014, announced its intention to mint its own currency in the parts of Iraq and Syria it had captured (Daragahi 2014). Banknotes have often been used to memorialize the achievements of famous male citizens of a given nation or territory, but female figures have more often been used to connote abstract qualities such as Freedom, Justice, and so on (Hewitt 1994). Money can also symbolize some qualitative aspect of a territory, whether real or imagined – when euro notes were designed, they could not refer to any of the member nations, and instead depicted a series of bridges, arches and doorways, with the intention of signalling connectedness rather than place (Fornas 2012). Similarly, as other currencies become de-linked from the nation – as in the case of alternative currencies such as Bitcoins, Starbucks Stars or Brixton Pounds[1] – notes, coins and other aspects of payment may come to symbolize some other form of identity or affiliation, linked to much smaller territorial units or no territory at all.

Psychoanalysis and money symbolism

Among the psychological sciences, the most intriguing elaborations of the symbolic aspects of money have come from psychoanalytic traditions. Unlike sociologists such as Simmel, who saw apparently 'personal' qualities like greed and parsimony as outgrowths of the development of the money system itself, the earliest works in psychoanalysis viewed attitudes to money as psychic elaborations of bodily functions. Freud and many of his followers initially saw parsimony as emerging from the sublimation in adult life of an anal-erotic phase from childhood. In this view, the link between money and 'anality', or 'the anal character', is the fact that faeces are one of the very few things over which young children can exert some control (Borneman 1976). Children learn fairly rapidly that this capacity can be used to please or frustrate their parents, and from the associated feeling of power they learn to derive some satisfaction.

As children grow up, these pleasures of control get transferred onto different kinds of objects, of which money, for many early analysts, was a prominent example.

In an alternative view, associated with Melanie Klein and her followers, attitudes of greed or envy in adult life (including those related to money and material goods) can be understood as symbolic elaborations of a more primal acquisitiveness. This acquisitiveness is related not to anal experience, but rather to the breast and the experience of suckling, feeding and being soothed. As Joan Rivière puts it, 'since to a baby well-being comes principally by means of its mouth and by milk, *the process of taking in and getting* acquires great significance to us as a means of warding off or ousting pain' (1964: 26, emphasis added). Greed – but by extension all forms of acquisitiveness – is therefore fundamentally an attempt to soothe anxiety and to defend against internal bad feelings of various kinds – a perspective that bears comparison with Schopenhauer's suggestion that satisfactions are always negative, in the sense that they are merely concerned with the elimination of a 'painful condition of deprivation' (Simmel 1978: 262).

For psychoanalytic writers working in a more relational idiom, the limitation to these approaches is that by fixing the meanings of money in particular bodily functions, one is liable to miss many details of the relationships and transactions within which particular attitudes to and uses of money come to the fore, and which give them their charge (although, as I suggest below, Freud himself noted a number of relational dimensions of money). Contemporary psychoanalytic writers, like sociologists, therefore typically see money as capable of symbolizing more than one thing, and assume that its meanings are to be discerned within the context of specific relationships. Some work has focused on the way that therapeutic clients may adopt a withholding attitude to fees – regularly being late paying, for example – as an attempt to control the therapist, and some suggest that certain patients seek 'special treatment' by vigorously resisting discussions of raising fees, out of an exaggerated sense of entitlement or deservingness (Valentine 1999; Gerrard 2002). In a case reported by Phillips (2006), a patient's father offers his therapist 'any money you want' in order to achieve certain outcomes for his son, which Phillips takes as an attempt to control a therapeutic process that is in fact out of his hands.

To say that the satisfactions of money are 'substitutes' or symbols – either for early bodily sensations or for the dynamics of relationships – does not mean that the materiality of money is irrelevant. In a technical essay on the payment of fees, Freud (1958 [1913]) implies that it is precisely *because* the presence or absence of money has real, and deeply felt, material consequences that it can be charged with so much symbolic significance. In this essay, Freud makes it clear that there are dangers for analysts in treating money as merely symbolic, or of 'act[ing] the part of the disinterested philanthropist' when setting the fee. If they are not honest about their own financial needs, and set the fee too low, they may become 'secretly aggrieved' at the patient, inhibiting their ability to help them. The patient, for their part, will not be inclined to value the treatment if the fee is too low. Indeed, offering the treatment for free – as one might do out of sympathy, or to remove an obstacle to progress – simply doesn't work, because it introduces an unhelpful new dynamic in the therapeutic relationship (the 'obligation to be grateful') that Freud suggests male patients in particular may object to and resist.

The symbolic function of payments

That money is never 'pure quantity', and that the advent of money does not reduce all qualitative difference to quantity, has been at the heart of Viviana Zelizer's work since her study of the social meaning of money (1994). Of particular interest here is her work on the relational and communicative dimension of payments. Contrary to critics such as Marx, who suggest that money corrupts relationships, Zelizer sees money and relationships as unavoidably intertwined. While it may be right, at the macro level, to point out that processes of commodification can structurally alter relationships in ways that have harmful side effects (as in some of the cases described by Sandel 2012), at the micro level of ordinary interactions the fact of monetary exchanges and obligations cannot simply be thought of as tainting a previously 'pure' realm of relating. Zelizer's view – which builds on a good deal of anthropological work (e.g., Parry and Bloch 1989) – is that no such pure realm exists. What is therefore more interesting for her is the way that people *manage* these unavoidable entanglements of intimacy and economy by using particular payment practices to say something about the nature of their ties – that is, to use the material structures and conventional practices surrounding money (monetary 'media') to communicate something about the relationship.

Money and payments in the context of close relationships are, for Zelizer, all about the cultural work of making 'viable matches' between the type of relationship and the payment arrangement (2012: 151–2). This is something that, to some degree, we all do instinctively, and it draws not just on individual judgement but wider cultural custom. Giving cash as a gift, for example, is not typically seen as appropriate – it may seem to violate a taboo by introducing quantity into an area that is increasingly treated as qualitative and 'beyond price'. On the other hand, there are certain contexts – and relationships – in which cash gifts signify differently. In the context of parent–child relationships, as noted above, giving cash may signify the continued willingness to help in times of financial need, but it may also be a way of acknowledging the child's freedom and autonomy, in place of earlier attempts to guide or shape. And in some countries giving cash at weddings or baptisms is a customary way of wishing good luck and prosperity.[2]

Zelizer's work echoes and builds upon earlier anthropological work that has explored at some length the question of money's power to corrupt. Parry and Bloch (1989) show that, contrary to Western theory's obsession with the idea of money as intrinsically revolutionary, anthropological studies suggest great cultural variability in the symbolism associated with it. Although anthropology itself has often been susceptible to the Western belief in the transformative power of money, and has thus tended to underplay the significance of money and market exchange in pre-capitalist societies, more recent studies suggest both the widespread importance of monetary exchanges in traditional economies, and the variable cultural customs built around such exchanges (pp. 7–8). Indeed, where writers like Simmel (and plenty of more recent commentators too) point to the potential for money to give rise to a particular worldview, Parry and Bloch's emphasis is on 'how an existing world view gives rise to particular ways of representing money' (p. 19):

> When the argument that money brings about a radical transformation of society is extended by the proposition that it must therefore lead to revolutionary and *specifiable* changes in world view, it is easy to further assume that money always means what money (supposedly) does. Regardless of culture, it will always tend to symbolise much the same kinds of things. But ... the meanings with which money is invested are quite as much a product of the cultural matrix into which it is incorporated as of the economic functions it performs ... It is therefore impossible to predict its symbolic meanings from these functions alone. (pp. 20–1)

Zelizer's argument builds on precisely this insight, and shows that the meanings with which money is invested vary according to the category of social relations in which it is embedded. Within a given type of relationship (e.g., a friendship group, parent–child relationships, patron–client relationships), some kinds of transactions will be deemed appropriate and others will be inappropriate; similarly, certain kinds of media will be suitable for those transactions and others will not (2005). Her notion of 'viable matches' in the realm of payments can also be usefully compared to work on the anthropology of communication. Madianou and Miller (2013), for example, coin the term 'polymedia' to suggest that in a hyper-mediated world of multiple platforms, media constitute a symbolic repertoire in their own right from which users can draw to add additional layers of meaning to their communications. Rather than seeing the absence of face-to-face communication as an inevitable impoverishment, they use the case of parents working abroad, and their communications with family back home, to show how people choose among various different communication options in ways that 'match' the nature of the conversation, the status of the relationship at a given time, or their feelings about topics being discussed. In this way, media use 'becomes part of relationship and emotional management' (2013: 171), and different media function for their interviewees in ways that mirror the use of payments in Zelizer's study: that is, as a means for symbolizing something about their relationship and communicating it.

The media of payments are also an important way in which the state symbolizes its relationship with its citizens and others in its care. On two occasions between 2000 and 2006, for example, the UK government made payments to those seeking asylum in the country using a voucher system that restricted their spending to food and drink in a limited number of supermarkets, and did not give them change. Refugee groups argued that, compared with cash payments, this system stigmatized asylum seekers, and thereby damaged community relations. Government research into the first version of the system found that many asylum seekers felt embarrassed using the vouchers and experienced hostility from other supermarket customers (Travis 2006). While denominated in the national currency, the use of a distinctive payment system here signified categorical differences in the nature of users' relationship to the nation-state, creating, in effect, a separate class of person with a demonstrably more restricted relationship to the use of the pound.

Another instance of the symbolic function of payments – again operating at a wider, social scale rather than in intimate relations – is the case of monetary payments for reparations or criminal sanctions. One particularly powerful illustration of the communicative capacity of money – as well as its complexity – comes from the case of compensation payments. As O'Malley (2009, 2011) argues, it is of great, if underappreciated, significance that money has come to be the predominant sanction in criminal, civil and regulatory law; the proliferation of monetary sanctions such as fines and damages has in many contexts tilted justice itself towards being a 'monetized apparatus for the pricing and distribution of risk' (2011: 547). The apparent 'meaninglessness' of money, he suggests, is part of what makes these developments possible, but to settle a claim through monetary payment can, paradoxically, itself be a highly significant act. Because fines can usually be paid 'by anyone on behalf of anyone', justice increasingly becomes separated from the individual wrongdoer. In fact, 'by requiring only that money be paid – by anyone – fines aim at *reducing probabilities of action* rather than seeking individual punishment or reform' (2011: 546–7, emphasis added). This can both expand the territory of regulation, and change the shape of justice.

In the case of state reparations for violence, payments have become a common part of human rights discourse, and are usually made explicitly in order to communicate something on the part of the wrongdoer – sorrow, apology, acknowledgement of harm, or perhaps a desire to move on (Moon 2013: 257). At the same time, those receiving such payments may read them as an attempt to 'buy their silence', or to signal that a matter of dispute is now closed, and that further discussion or argument is not warranted. In some cases, the explicitly symbolic, rather than economic, nature of reparations payments is precisely the problem: as Clare Moon shows in the case of apartheid South Africa, the decision of the Truth and Reconciliation Committee (TRC) to pursue symbolic reparations payments rather than monetary ones was contentious because it was deemed by some to leave the severe material inequalities caused by apartheid unaddressed, and ignored the role of multinational corporations who had benefited economically from the system (Moon 2013: 264). That some South Africans pursued claims for compensation against multinational corporations was in this sense a way of drawing attention to the real material costs of apartheid but also a way of saying something different about their experience – something not necessarily captured by the formal TRC process.

The meaning of price

A common theme in all these cases is that although money seems to be a matter of pure quantity (Simmel 1978), it is often replete with qualitative aspects. This is not just true of the decorated notes and coins that 'stand in for' the money system, but also for money as amount. In a study of money and numbering practices, Jane Guyer (2004), for example, shows that trade in West Africa has at various points in history endowed quantities with symbolic dimensions. In many contexts, she says, 'quantity was *a form of quality*':

> Number and kind were both scales, among others; none was anchored in a foundational invariant; all were at play. Quantity was a form of power, available for use as a qualitative weapon, as when amounts in circulation were deliberately driven either high or low enough to cross quite-well-understood thresholds of function or conception. (2004: 12)

There were certain 'benchmark' or 'tropic' numbers – twenty, for example, or two hundred – that took on a qualitative significance because they were thresholds at which quantity intersected with other ways of organizing and ranking the world, such as prizes and titles (Guyer 2010). Something similar can be found in various contemporary commercial contexts, where particular numbers or multiples are found to have a higher-than-expected frequency. The use of the number ninety-nine in pricing, for example, means that it, too, has taken on a 'tropic' quality; elsewhere, the higher-than-expected frequency of sixes and their multiples has been attributed to their prevalence in trading contexts such as the packaging of eggs or bottles of wine (Coupland 2011: 35).

Prices can be communicative or symbolic in other ways too. There is some evidence that people prefer round numbers in everyday contexts where there is a need for ease of use and manipulation, and where the demand for precision is low (Coupland 2011). Yet in commercial contexts round numbers may be read quite differently: research from the ride-sharing platform Uber found that people distrusted its 'surge pricing' multiple when it was a round number, and were less inclined to book a ride when the multiple was 2.0 than when it was 2.1 (Dahl 2016). The implication was that the round number appeared to consumers to be the result of human agency, rather than the output of an algorithm processing 'objective' data about the state of the market. There is an understandable comfort in the feeling that the market is impersonal, and that the same algorithm is being used for everyone, because historically the depersonalization of exchange, and the anonymity of mass-market society, has been seen as a countervailing force against the potential for discrimination in face-to-face bargaining contexts.

Perhaps the most famous examples of price's communicative function are found in the practices of 'psychological' pricing by marketers. These include the 'Veblen effect', in which part of the utility of a good is said to derive from the price paid for it, and indeed in which increases in price may increase, rather than decrease, demand. What is at stake here is again that price is precisely *not* just quantitative information but is 'valued as a cultural signal' (Beckert and Aspers 2011: 10). But it is not just at the upper end of the pricing spectrum that psychological pricing works: marketers recognize that price can be a communicative force in its own right, rather than simply the outcome of supply and demand. This means that it can be used to shape the market and to segment customers into groups, and thereby to shape 'reference prices' – the prices 'that buyers carry in their minds and refer to when looking at a given product' (Kotler and Armstrong 2014: 341) – at all kinds of price points. The manipulation of price is thus a way for companies to send a signal about a brand or product's positioning, and to specify who it is for.

Prices can also gain their symbolic resonance through the narratives and stories used to contextualize them: in the case described by Velthuis (2005), on pricing in the art world, dealers develop stories or 'scripts' to justify and explain prices. As I will explore further in chapter 5, these narratives might contextualize prices by talking about an 'honourable' art world falling prey to capitalism, or about the fame and stardom of a particular artist explaining increasing prices for their work, or conversely by saying that a cautious or 'prudent' approach to pricing reflects the care a gallery expresses for the building of an artist's career over the long term. Taken together, Velthuis shows how the prices for artworks, and the way these are talked about, can be used to symbolize or signify something about the artist, something about the art world or something about the dealer.

Changing meanings of money, payment and price

Let me turn now to consider some of the ways in which the symbolic properties of money, payments and pricing are changing. Perhaps the most obvious development to note is the rise of alternative or non-state currencies, including local currencies, cryptocurrencies and special purpose currencies such as loyalty points or club memberships. These challenge the hegemony of fiat, or state-backed, currencies, and offer a new set of symbolic associations based on such things as community and location, political opposition, affinity to a brand and so on. Above all, alternative currencies tend to express non-national forms of social collectivity. Thus in the case of alternative and local currencies (which could include both genuine 'alternatives' to money, such as time banking, or alternative currencies that can only be used in a restricted set of venues), one motivation has historically been financial inclusion – a way for people to participate in exchange even if they don't have much money (see Hart

2001) – but another has been to assert the primacy of local businesses, and local people's needs, over those of large companies from elsewhere. Keeping economic transactions tied to a local network is a way of using money as a medium to facilitate and protect community, but also a way of symbolizing that community both to insiders and outsiders.

In the case of cryptocurrencies, the underlying political rationale for their founding has been one of the main sources of their symbolism. The development and use of Bitcoin were tied up with the assertion of a critical attitude towards the nation-state, and towards the private companies and payment intermediaries who sometimes operate as proxies for them. One of the motivations for the creation of Bitcoin, as Maurer et al. (2013) note, was anger at governments' reaction to the financial crisis of 2007–8, but more specifically at the role of banks and other private sector payment intermediaries. In addition to extracting profits through their monopoly on transactions, these intermediaries were also held responsible for invading people's privacy, and in some cases for using their power to censor organizations or shut them down by freezing payments to them under pressure from the US government. A pervasive sense that governments may exercise power arbitrarily, and that private sector actors are even less accountable, is a strong motivation for the formulation and use of alternative forms of payment. These founding logics mean that cryptocurrencies have – at least for now – been able to retain some of the symbolism and connotations of radicalism and autonomy, even as they are used less as an alternative to fiat currency and much more like just another speculative asset.

In fact, the symbolism of autonomy from state and commercial mediation associated with alternative currencies may not be such a benign development as some proponents suggest. The potential to create multiple currencies – perhaps based on location, or shared affinities and values – may emerge from 'the shared desire to minimise transaction costs for "us" at the possible expense of transaction costs for "them"' (Birch 2014: 97). But it may in fact introduce new forms of discrimination and division into the realm of exchange, on top of those that exist already. At the very least, it is likely to introduce new transaction costs (see Kaminska 2017), even while it potentially diminishes the ability of one or two very powerful firms to control profit from fees. And it is not necessarily clear that allowing people to bypass the state entirely is a good idea in the longer run. In less optimistic accounts of the future, the growth of 'wildcat' and other private currencies (Castronova 2015) is threatening precisely because it may break the link between individuals and the state, hollowing out the state's capacity to act in the interest of community (e.g., by levying taxes), and giving people less and less reason to feel invested in, or connected to, those most proximate to them (Spang 2015).

In another development, the symbolism of money and payments is being subtly reworked by the decline of some traditional media of exchange and the rise of new ones. In particular, the smaller proportion of payments now made in cash suggests that the official symbolism of state currency, as something experienced in small, repetitive ways in everyday life, may be declining and being replaced with different forms of symbolism associated with payments cards, wearable devices and phone apps. Of course, state-issued coins and notes have never monopolized the symbolism of payments media either: earlier, private currencies and in the twentieth century debit and credit cards have also had symbolic properties (Langley 2008; Swartz 2014). These external markers of the line of credit available to a given person may well continue in some form. At the same time, these externally imposed distinctions can increasingly be augmented or cross cut with more individual forms of expression, such as choice of card colour or choice of a favourite picture.

However, when payment is no longer made through a card issued by a bank, but rather via a phone or other portable device, some aspects of payment symbolism become subsumed into other aspects of the person – for example, shifting from banking brands to technology or social media brands. A related tendency associated with digital money and payments is towards public display of the social networks in which transactions are embedded. As Lana Swartz (2020) notes in her work on 'transactional communities', applications like Venmo, at least in their initial stage, were developed to put payments and money transfers into the context of a social media-like system, with a 'feed' that posted information about the payments made by other contacts. These restricted groupings may be more 'private' than showing everyone in a store your American Express Platinum card (or, in the case of asylum seekers in the UK described above, in being forced to use payments that mark you as different from other members of a polity). Yet in other ways these kinds of systems entail much greater public exposure of previously unobservable transactions, potentially turning payment into an opportunity for performance.

Indeed, it is worth noting that some innovations in the realm of banking and payments entail significant shifts in the way that information is gathered and shared. In the UK, the 'open banking' initiative, which aimed to encourage the growth of financial start-ups in order to dilute the dominance of traditional providers, has led to the emergence of a range of 'challenger banks' and non-banking 'fintech' providers. These often offer new or enhanced payment facilities, such as easily transferring money abroad, or making payments using other currency denominations, but they do so within a business model that allows the sharing (and sale) of personal data in ways that were not the case for traditional banks (see Hickey 2018). One 'challenger bank', Revolut, caused controversy in 2019 with a series of advertisements suggesting that their customer spending data was sufficiently granular to identify consumers who had bought a vegan sausage roll from the bakery Greggs in the previous month (Barrett 2019). This turned out to be an exaggeration, but it alerted many to the sheer volume of data that banks and credit card providers hold about consumers, and about the new potential – via 'open banking' – to share that data with third parties. These kinds of developments mean that while changes in the 'payments space' (Maurer 2012) may be moving some aspects of payment away from *public* visibility associated with the signifying properties of credit cards or private banks, they may be moving towards at least two new forms of visibility: one, grounded in social networks, where payment becomes just like any other kind of action that can be shared on social media; and two, a new type of 'private' visibility – to those willing to pay – grounded in the collection and sale of data, and the availability of one's spending information in areas far beyond banking. These kinds of developments point to the continued salience of forms of monetary distinction and differentiation, even in contexts where digitization appears to make transactions less visible and tangible. We have already seen arguments that social identities, perhaps organized around place or affinity, may form the basis for future innovations in money and currency (Birch 2014). However, it is also clear that other innovations are based on the trade of information.

Data and information are also central to changes in the areas of price and pricing, and these in turn have implications for price's signifying properties. As I have argued above, it is rarely the case that price only signifies the state of supply and demand; not only does it reflect the various social factors that have gone into its calculation (see, e.g., Beckert 2011; Moor and Lury 2018; McFall and Moor 2019), it can also be adjusted in order to say something about the good or service on offer – that is, it can be used as part of marketing – and the numbers used in pricing often have qualitative, even tropic, significance. Historically the capacity of prices to 'speak' or signify beyond the mere transmission of information has been tied to the fact that prices are usually *public*, the same for everyone. Although fixed, public and openly displayed prices are a relatively recent development in historical terms, they have been a stable feature of most commercial environments for more than a hundred years (Carrier 1994). This is now beginning to change. In its place, we are witnessing the rise of dynamic, personalized, private and, in some cases, constantly fluctuating pricing. How will this alter the capacity of price to symbolize or signify?

Current changes in pricing technology are interesting in part because they simultaneously allow price to become *more* like it is in market theory – that is, a reflection of the state of supply and demand – but also much less like it at the same time. On the one hand, there are examples of pricing systems where price changes frequently to reflect how the market is functioning. These include the 'fluctuating' pricing systems used by car rental services such as Uber and Lyft. These are designed to provide a real-time indication of the state of the market, and to encourage drivers in particular to offer their services when supply is low and demand (and therefore price) is high. In this respect, technology facilitates a more efficient market. The same logic is at work in energy systems that use in-home devices to show energy price changes to consumers in real time. This is particularly the case in the market for renewable energy, where it is costly for firms to store the energy for long periods. Firms typically want to even out demand, and thus can constantly vary the prices offered to consumers to incentivize use when demand is low and to discourage use when demand is highest. Finally, there is also some evidence that supermarkets are experimenting with the possibilities of 'live' or constantly fluctuating prices (Morley 2017). This would allow them to more easily dispense with unwanted stock – being potentially quicker than discounting everything by hand – but also to exploit surges in demand, such as those associated with sudden bursts of hot or cold weather.

And yet the data collected about individuals is now so diffuse in nature, and the capacity to target people at an individual or micro level so advanced, that all manner of factors beyond supply and demand can now be included in a price. Some examples of this are the ability to track browsing history, so that a vendor may potentially know the price of similar goods you have recently looked at, purchase behaviour, or even – relevant to some kinds of purchases – how much phone battery you have remaining. In most cases vendors can also easily know what type of device or software you are using to access a site, with some studies finding that users of Apple devices are charged more (Valentino-Devries et al. 2012), and some kinds of transactions or searches also involve postcodes (or zip codes), which again have been used in price variation strategies (Vafa et al. 2015). These types of information allow vendors to make inferences about consumers' 'reservation prices', or the maximum they are willing to pay. They can then try to steer consumers towards a particular price (by showing search results that are skewed towards a particular price bracket), or engage in price discrimination or personalization, where an individual price is calculated on the basis of these various inputs and inferences, and, in principle, a different price could be offered to every consumer. The proprietary nature of the systems used to make such calculations means that it is extremely hard for any one individual to know which elements have gone into the price they are being offered.

These changes in pricing technology may have significant implications for how price signifies or symbolizes. In Hayek's formulation, price was like a 'telecommunications system' because it allowed people to quickly see what was going on elsewhere in the market. It allowed people to see the state of supply and demand and by implication what other people were doing. And yet, although new pricing technologies have the potential to do this more effectively than ever before, in reality it will be much harder to believe that price reflects a market 'out there'; we will be increasingly aware that the price we see does not only reflect data about the market, but also the personal data that has been collected about us. In other words, price may not simply reflect supply and demand, but rather what a company believes is the maximum price we are willing or able to pay. This may, as Joseph Turow (2006) has suggested, lead to a situation of 'envy and suspicion in the public sphere', with the *lack* of certainty about what price signifies leaving people wondering how they are ranked by corporations and whether others are being treated preferentially. Price discrimination, practised at any wide scale, puts an end to the idea that 'my money's as good as anyone else's', with potential consequences not just for trust in corporations but for the credibility of an ideology that markets are fair and non-discriminatory places.

Conclusion

In this chapter I have mapped some of the ways in which the idea of economic action as communicative is approached in the social sciences. In identifying various symbolic aspects of money and payment – currency symbolism, psychoanalytic theories of money, the relational meanings of payments and payment types, the symbolism of quantity and the signifying properties of price and pricing – my aim has been to show that there are diverse, powerful ways of thinking about how communication functions in economic life beyond those from economics, or from the more traditional media and communications approaches of political economy or the study of media texts. To focus on communication as symbolism and signification is, instead, to take an ethnographic or anthropological turn, a move that draws attention not only to the work of representing or debating or informing, but also to the work of making a coherent and meaningful world that we can inhabit, and understanding how others have done the same (Geertz 1973; Carey 1989: 85).

Symbolism, understood in this way, is a medium or a mechanism for social integration. By the same token, however, it can also be a force for social division, classification and exclusion. This can be true at the individual level, as evidenced in the ways we use money and payments differently to make distinctions between closer or more distant personal ties. However, social divisions may also be imposed on us from the outside, as for example when credit card providers make differences in wealth and therefore credit availability public in the form of card symbolism. Divisions may also be sanctioned by the state, as in the example of the UK government making those seeking asylum use different payment systems to other citizens.

None of the possible changes in the symbolic properties of money, payment and price that I have outlined in the second part of this chapter look likely to resolve this historical tension between money's power to unite and generate collectivity, and its power to divide and exclude (see Spang 2016). In the most optimistic accounts of the future of money (e.g., Hart 2001; Birch 2014), a proliferation of independent currencies, facilitated by the internet and digital media, will make it more and more possible for ordinary people to take control of their economic lives. In this view, the ability to process and record large amounts of data about transactions will form part of the context for a 're-personalization' of economic life, and people will increasingly be able to designate their own money of account, perhaps tied to locality or community, and not necessarily linked to a national currency (Hart 2001: 278–9). This in turn will 'extend considerably our capacities to buy and sell without relying on some exogenous source of employment ... to finance our activities', and should 'extend the range of economic activities that individuals can participate in, if the wider market economy does not yield them the money they need' (pp. 281–2).

Yet there are reasons to be cautious about what this might look like in practice. If money is a medium for social integration, as Habermas and others have argued, and part of the way 'imagined communities' are formed, the proliferation of private or territorial currencies is likely to lead to divisions, even if, as proponents suggest, it also multiplies the lines of credit and resources available to people. And as Hart (2001) acknowledges, the same technology that potentially transfers more power and agency to consumers can also be used to target them more carefully, singling out the wealthiest consumers for special treatment and ignoring or rejecting those deemed insufficiently valuable. From this perspective, one possibility is that 'personalization' will, in effect, mean a return to different currencies – or at least, substantially different monetary experiences – for rich and poor (see also Spang 2016). At the heart of the forms of personalization currently being developed by commercial actors are ever more nimble, but also increasingly opaque, forms of classification, which are made on the basis of complex and shifting variables of which users themselves may have little awareness. In this form of personalization, what is at stake is in fact the isolation of consumers from other market actors, depriving them of any kind of overview of market activity and of information about the prices paid by other consumers. In this respect, the pricing and payment systems organized by large corporations with proprietary databases of transaction data have the potential to significantly disrupt the symbolic connections between the individual and the collective that national currencies and fixed, open prices made possible.

Money's communicative capacities are tied to many things, but among the most important are community, connection and collectivity. This harks back to an ancient association between 'communication' and 'communion'; as James Carey (1989: 18) puts it, communication in this view is oriented 'not toward the extension of messages in space, but toward the maintenance of society in time'. Currency, payments and prices may 'send a message' but they do this less in the sense of transmitting information and more in the sense of asserting and reasserting bonds between the individual and the collective, or – as we have seen in some examples in this chapter – rejecting those links and attempting to create new ones. As forms of money and payment evolve, they are likely to face many of the same tensions that can be traced throughout monetary history: between state or corporate power on the one hand and the autonomy and privacy of ordinary people on the other, and between money's power to generate collectivity and its power to divide and exclude.

Part II

Communication constructs economic life

In this second part of the book, the focus shifts away from the communicative nature of specific economic actions, and towards a broader assessment of how modalities of communication construct economic life. I take four types of communication (promotion, information, narrative and discussion) and explore the ways they shape our economic lives, from the language used by economists and central bankers to promotion and self-promotion at work, and from online consumer reviews and discussions to the stories told about money and relationships in films and novels. This variety of cases is important because the role of communication in economic life is often studied in rather narrow ways. Within the field of media and communications, for example, people often look either at macroeconomic news coverage or at consumer-facing advertisements; within economic sociology there is a growing focus on how 'culture' (broadly conceived) shapes economic institutions and actions, but surprisingly little interest in communication per se. There is not much sense, in either of these traditions, of the varieties of communicative material that make up our ordinary economic activities, and, as a result, the much wider range of ways in which communication shapes our economic lives goes mostly unaccounted for.

The forms of communication I consider in this part of the book – promoting, informing, narrating and discussing – necessarily represent just a small selection of the communicative forms that make up economic life. They have been chosen to correspond loosely to different rhetorical modes (i.e., argumentation, exposition, narration and description), and as such their scope is quite broad, but due to limitations of space they inevitably present only a partial picture of economic communication. I hope the reader will be able to imagine for themselves how one might take the logic of this part of the book and extend it to include other varieties of communication (such as gossip and rumour), other instances of narrating, promoting, discussing or informing, or more situationally specific genres of communication (such as workplace meetings or bank statements).

A key reason for focusing on varieties of communication, rather than specific media, is to avoid the media-centric trap of assuming that media (or 'the media') are the most important parts of everyday life, or that mediated forms of communication are inherently more powerful or consequential than non-mediated ones. My aim instead has been to foreground a broader understanding of communication, and to capture the ways that different *purposive* forms of communication contribute to the construction of economic life, while leaving open the question of the extent to which *media* of different kinds are necessary to how these forms of communication function. As we shall see, some elements of the communicative ordering of economic life discussed in these four chapters come from mass media institutions, while others work through smaller media channels, and others function primarily through face-to-face or other 'live' forms of communication that are mediated only by voice, material or language.

Finally, although the remaining chapters of the book entail a shift of focus, the reader will find that some of the themes from Part I do emerge again, albeit in slightly different form. For example, the 'economic' understandings of communication outlined in chapter 1 appear again in chapter 4, where online commerce and digital platforms often both assume and enact understandings of communication as information (or even more simply, 'data'), and treat consumer actions as observable data points that can be used to infer preferences or intentions. Similarly, the ideas discussed in chapter 2 – that currencies, prices and payments can all be construed as 'communicative' as well as symbolic – appear again in chapter 5 in discussions of the way that money is represented in fiction, in chapter 6 where I consider online discussions about money and relationships, and in chapter 4 where I revisit the topic of alternative currencies.

Chapter 3

Promotion

In the remaining chapters of the book, my focus turns towards specific *modes* of communication and their contribution to economic life. The first I consider is promotion. Promotion is often seen as a quintessentially 'economic' form of communication because many of its most obvious forms are tied to profit seeking. And, indeed, academic scholarship on promotion does often focus on the advertising and marketing activities of firms, and on the promotion of commodities in a capitalist market. But my starting point in this chapter is that making money, or making a profit, is in fact only one of a number of possible outcomes sought by persuasive or self-advancing (or self-advantaging) communication; others include the pursuit of power, prestige or influence, or the promotion of a particular idea, belief or point of view. The term 'promotion' has quite legitimately acquired many meanings and associations over time, from simply 'drawing attention to something' to more profound efforts to manipulate or persuade through deception. We can correspondingly find evidence of promotional or persuasive communication across all areas of economic life: not just in the advertising campaigns of powerful brands, but also in the ideological outpourings of partisan newspapers and the utterances of politicians and bankers, to the more banal instances of self-promotion on social media or in our working lives.

Promotion is a form of communication that operates simultaneously along several axes, and this means it is hard to definitively separate it from related terms like persuasion or propaganda. In order to analyse promotional communication, it is therefore useful to bring these various axes to the foreground. First, promotion can be more or less self-advancing. As we shall see, the promotion of economic ideas or goals sometimes entails *self*-advancement for the speaker, or the promotion of a particular ideology or viewpoint, but it may also include some more disinterested elements, or a partial intention to advance *collective* understanding. Next, promotion can be more or less open to debate or dissent; at one extreme it may be more like a dialogue, with (for example) a politician promoting one view of the economy, and their opponents offering others. At the other extreme, 'speaking back' to promotion may be so hard that it is more like the propaganda of an authoritarian regime. In the middle lie many commercial forms of promotion, such as advertisements, which do not explicitly invite a dialogue or response (although the search for customer 'engagement' is changing this), but which may nonetheless find themselves at the heart of a controversy where they are challenged or criticized. Finally, promotion can be more or less hidden. In some of the cases of 'delinguistified communication' described at the end of the chapter, the aim is not just to bypass dialogue and discussion, but also to avoid conscious acknowledgement or recognition altogether. Yet at the other end of the spectrum there remain many forms of promotion that quite plainly announce themselves as such, and while they do not invite debate, nor do they seek to hide their persuasive intent.

The breadth and diversity of promotional communication is reflected in the topics I cover in the rest of this chapter. First, I examine the contribution of promotion to economic life at the level of rhetoric. The language and linguistic devices used to describe the economy are powerfully promotional, from the language of academic economists trying to persuade readers of the secure, scientific basis of their arguments, to the speeches of central bank staff or the pronouncements of politicians at budget time. Next, I consider the function of promotion in the world of work. Here promotion constructs economic life in at least two ways: there is, on the one hand, the sheer number of jobs that now involve promotion as one of their components; but there is also an increasing role for *self-promotion*, even in jobs whose ostensible focus has little or nothing to do with persuasion. Widely seen as inevitable or even necessary, I show that self-promotion at work often has more to do with institutional failings than with any 'natural' disposition to promote or persuade.

Finally, I return to the promotion of consumer goods and brands, but examine a form of promotion that has historically received less attention than advertising or PR. This is the sphere of 'delinguistified' communication, a term I take from Habermas (1987) to refer to various mute or non-linguistic forms of communication, such as those included in product design, the design of spaces and buildings, the architecture of websites and the design of interfaces, or the branding of uniforms, delivery vans and so on. These types of promotion are in many ways typical of contemporary strategic communication, since they are both ubiquitous and tend to conceal their strategic intent. As well as being non-linguistic, these forms of communication are also importantly non-discursive and non-dialogic.

The implications of this are to make promotional communication harder to identify, but also harder to avoid or dispute. The broader significance of this tendency in contemporary promotion is discussed at the end of the chapter.

The rhetoric of the economic system

Prehistories of promotion can be found in many places: in religious iconography, political propaganda or the art of rhetoric. Rhetoric is a useful place to start, because debates about rhetoric – in essence, the attempt to persuade and influence by linguistic means – have historically been very good at capturing promotion's ambiguity. Debates often revolve around the question of whether rhetoric is 'a neutral tool for bringing about agreements, or an immoral activity that ends in manipulation and deception' (Herrick 2009: 3). And this debate, in turn, typically hinges on the nature of persuasion and how it is accomplished: as studies of rhetoric show, persuasion does not only involve rational argument ('reasoning made public') and the invitation to engage in dialogue, but also emotional appeals of various kinds, and the careful planning or manipulation of aesthetic elements in order to influence. As such, rhetoric seems to combine modes of communication – the rational and the strategic – that, in more modern accounts of media and communication, are usually treated as separate (e.g., Habermas 1984).

The ambivalent nature of persuasive communication thus comes in part from the fact that it combines modes of discourse that scholars would often rather keep apart. But it is also a matter of the uses to which it is put: rhetoric and persuasion can be used for 'seeking cooperation ... building a consensus ... [and] wishing to be understood', but also for 'gaining compliance', 'having the last word' (Herrick 2009: 3, 10–11) and simply getting people to change their behaviour in one's own interests. In some cases, rhetoric may be more or less synonymous with deliberation – or what Habermas (1984: 286) would call an action oriented to mutual understanding. In other cases, it may be entirely strategic: an 'action oriented to success'. While Habermas himself understood that such 'pure' types of action were 'merely limit cases', the distinction has been vitally important in communications theory, and it is certainly useful in the practical matter of judging the various kinds of economic communication that are the subject of this book. If forms of economic communication that seem to be oriented towards clarity and understanding are in fact better construed as a concealed strategic action of some kind, this has consequences not only for the wider information environment, but also potentially for people's economic wellbeing.

One of the first ways in which rhetoric matters for the economy is at the very broad level of how economic life is framed and understood. Economic writing is a case in point. Deirdre McCloskey (1983) famously described economic writing as a form of rhetoric, pointing out that the commitment to the scientific (or 'modernist') method adopted from physics, led to certain trademark forms of argument. These included, most notably, a reliance on mathematical formulae and the demonstration of mathematical virtuosity, and heavy use of metaphors that 'convey the authority of Science, and often ... its claims to ethical neutrality' (1983: 500, 508). The demonstration of skill at mathematics was 'itself an important and persuasive argument' (p. 500), comparable to the way that skill at Latin or Greek might have seemed to qualify English men of the nineteenth century to be imperial leaders. In pointing this out, McCloskey's argument was not that economics should attempt to purge all rhetorical elements; it would be impossible to do so, since metaphor is essential to thought. Rather, her suggestion was that both the 'official' and more 'workaday' forms of rhetoric used in academic economic writing tended to get in the way of reflection and scrutiny, precisely because they were so taken for granted: the tacitness of much economic knowledge was unrecognized, and this led to teaching that proceeded through 'axiom and proof instead of by problem-solving and practice' (p. 513). 'The purpose of literary scrutiny', then, would be 'to see beyond the received view of its content' (p. 499).

Others have been more overtly critical than McCloskey, in part because they do not see the rhetoric as so benign. When Hayek spoke of the 'slavish imitation of the method and language of Science' (1942: 269) by economists and other social scientists, he was in part alluding to the tendency for the language of rational argument and demonstration to be invaded by other rhetorical devices (including the use of mathematical formulae) designed to persuade through appeals to authority or superior ability. Similarly, Mirowski (1989) has documented the problems that follow from an over-reliance on metaphors imported more or less wholesale from the physical sciences. Neither of these writers would dispute the idea that economic writing ought to persuade its audience. John Maynard Keynes famously used his journalistic writings to persuade, and to lay the groundwork for his economic theories, which were themselves often strongly rhetorical (Parsons 1989; see also Hart 2009), while Marxist ideology critique was designed to carefully *but persuasively* reveal and debunk bourgeois understandings of the economy. Rather, the claim of those critics would be that the *means* and the *intentions* of persuasion matter a great deal. When the self-advancing urge to 'win' (or to gain status through association with prestigious scientific disciplines) starts to impinge upon the aim of furthering understanding, rhetoric becomes strategic action rather than 'true' communication. In practice, of course, these aims and impulses can be difficult to disentangle.[1]

Promotional and persuasive logics can be found in much institutional discourse about the economy too. Catherine Walsh's study of UK chancellors' budget statements from the late 1970s until 2007 shows that, over time, these official statements came to '*publicize* … the idea of finance as an individual and public good' (2015: 67, emphasis added). Budget statements combine details about technical changes to economic organization with the signalling of a government's broad intentions and priorities. In the case of finance, Walsh shows that budget statements from 1979 onwards specified the state's direct support for the sale of financial products, but also included an 'indirect, *public-relations* side … in which the state insists that the financial sector is good for everyone's needs and desires' (2015: 68, emphasis added). Budget rhetoric, she suggests, signalled to London's financial district that City investment would be 'privileged, promoted and protected' (p. 73); at the same time, it also often 'preached' the virtues of share ownership and financial activity to a wider public.

A similarly promotional tone can be seen in central bank communications. Something like the Bank of England's CPI forecast is not just descriptive of likely changes in the level of consumer price inflation, but also of the intentions of the bank itself. As such, its intended function is precisely *not* just to describe, but also, as Douglas Holmes (2014: 24–5) puts it, 'to shape expectations … such that the market and the public will adjust their behavior'. Thus, the chart 'should be understood as a policy instrument designed to *influence the course of price behavior prospectively*, rather than serve as a pure, probabilistic representation of future conditions' (emphasis added), while the general challenge for central banks is to 'shape expectations with persuasive narratives'. For Holmes, this is an example of a particular kind of performativity: i.e., a representational practice that also constitutes what it describes. But it is also an example of promotion and persuasion, because it involves an attempt to propagate an idea and to 'pro-mote' – in the sense of anticipating and moving ahead of (Wernick 1991: 182) – a particular course of action.

In a more unusual form of central bank promotion, the Bank of Jamaica in 2019 and 2020 released a series of reggae and dancehall videos literally singing the virtues of 'low and stable inflation'.[2] In one, a stable inflation rate is described as being 'what the bassline is to reggae music'. In another, dancehall star Denyque describes how a stable inflation rate provides a solid basis for private sector activity, against a backdrop of construction vehicles and ports. As Clea Bourne[3] observes, these videos reflect the central bank's role as 'economic storyteller-in-chief', but they may also reflect some degree of nudging by the finance ministry, who want the public to be aware of the government's economic achievements, and want investors on global capital markets to see Jamaica as an appealing financial destination. They are thus partly a celebration of the country's macroeconomic stability after a long period of IMF monitoring, and partly a way of promoting Jamaica on global capital markets by showing that the central bank is actively engaged in targeting inflation and promoting growth. It has also been suggested that catchy songs and videos are the bank's way of anchoring the public's expectations of what inflation 'should' be, as a kind of inoculation against 'irresponsible politics' in the future.

What makes these forms of communication about the economic system promotional is that the impulse to promote and influence, and not simply to inform, describe or clarify, is at their heart. For this reason, their choice of language is particularly important, and here metaphor holds a powerful place. Given the relatively low level of understanding of macroeconomic processes among the general population of most countries, the choice of metaphor for describing economic actions is important because it is a way of describing one thing – often something unfamiliar or poorly understood – in terms of something else (usually something more familiar or accessible). When politicians describe the state of the economy, or challenges facing the economy, it is therefore highly consequential if they use, say, a meteorological metaphor rather than a mechanical one. In the US, Barack Obama became president in 2008 at a time of a global financial crisis; in 2010 he gave a speech in which he made clear that the blame for this lay elsewhere, claiming that 'some folks ... drove our car into the ditch' (Obama 2010). In the UK, on the other hand, the chancellor of the exchequer George Osborne gave a speech to the Conservative Party conference in which he said that the nation would 'ride out the storm' of the financial crisis together, and 'move into the calmer, brighter seas beyond' (see Porter 2011). These offer quite different ideas about the nature of the financial crisis (a mechanical failure versus a natural phenomenon) but also, crucially, about responsibility for it. A car driven into a ditch is the result of bad driving – and perhaps, if one wants to spread out responsibility, a badly maintained road – but a storm is not something that anyone could have prevented, even if a good meteorologist might perhaps have seen it coming. It may seem something of a stretch to describe these metaphors as 'promotional', but the point is that these characterizations are not neutral: they do not simply describe or represent, but also advance and *advocate* a particular point of view on the state of the economic system and who is responsible for it.

The world of work: promotion and self-promotion

Let me now move away from the promotional rhetoric of economists and politicians to the slightly more familiar territory of work. Promotional communication penetrates the world of work in at least two ways, but let me start with the most obvious: promotion and persuasion are not simply 'texts' or 'outputs' that seek to stimulate economic exchange; they are also jobs and industries that employ large numbers of people. It has been estimated that promotion and persuasion make up between 25 and 30 per cent of the GDP of the United States (Antioch 2013; see also McCloskey and Klamer 1995). These figures reflect the fact that 'brand names, commercial trademarks and other intellectual property are playing a bigger role in economic transactions' (Antioch 2013: 8), but they also highlight the fact that promotion and persuasion are key components of many kinds of jobs. Indeed, by including lawyers, journalists and shop assistants in their list of promotional and persuasive professions, these figures remind us that promotion is not just a discrete industry or occupation, but also a mode of communication embedded in many aspects of work. Describing some of these jobs as 'promotional' may seem extravagant, but for reasons I will come to below, I suggest that this way of approaching promotional work actually provides a much more realistic account of the place of persuasive communication in our economic lives. In fact, this measure may even underplay the extent of promotion, since GDP often does not capture many of the economic exchanges (and associated forms of promotion and persuasion) that take place online (Coyle 2016).

We can, then, think of promotion as a set of industries or occupations that exert an influence on everything else (and whose influence may or may not be growing); or we can think of promotion as a form of communication embedded in many types of activity. The latter view is, for me, more credible. I share with Andrew Wernick the view that promotion is not simply a type of message, but 'a type of speech and, beyond that ... a *whole communicative function*' (1991: 181, emphasis added). I also share his view that 'all manner of communicative acts have, as one of their dimensions, and often only tacitly, the function of advancing some kind of self-advantaging exchange' (1991: 182). However, whereas Wernick often seems to attribute the ubiquity of promotion to a generalized consumerism, I am less convinced that asserting these origins is accurate or helpful. Given what we know about classical rhetoric as a site for deception, manipulation and flattery as well as rational persuasion, and the clear antecedents of contemporary promotion in forms of political propaganda and religious communication, advertising cannot be seen as the sole prototype for contemporary promotional communication. The more important point, I think, is that promotion is not limited to the commercial world, and that promotional modes of communication are common in 'non- or quasi-commercial forms of promotional practice' (1991: 192). As an example, Rebecca Bramall (2016) has shown how the movement for 'tax justice' in the UK has included a variety of activities that blur the line between traditional activism (e.g., awareness-raising about tax avoidance or the occupation of buildings) and public relations-style promotional stunts (e.g., hashtag campaigns and the occupation of Twitter feeds). There are important normative questions for activists about the tactics they use and – for example – how much hiddenness, self-interest or public debate is appropriate in any given campaign. But social media campaigns have been a political tool for at least as long as they have been a commercial one, and persuasive communication has not been imported into politics from the outside.

The blending of promotion into multiple activities can be seen in other areas too. In Antioch's account, for example, the roles of shop assistants are substantially promotional. This has in fact been documented in a number of studies: in Lynne Pettinger's (2004) study of UK retail workers, she shows that assistants are to varying degrees required to embody the values of the brand and promote these to customers through dress, body language, styles of helping and so on. Similarly, Christine Williams's (2006) study of toy stores in the US found that workers were often hired for customer-facing roles because their appearance or demeanour was felt to be consistent with the brand's 'values' or identity, something also traced elsewhere (Moor and Littler 2008). Importantly, these kinds of promotion-led hiring decisions in retail can easily shade into discrimination, since they tend to take relatively fixed bodily attributes (such as age, ethnicity and perceived attractiveness) as the basis for employment, seeing in those attributes some kind of promotional advantage for the brand.

More recently, Brooke Erin Duffy (2016) has shown that many of the newer types of labour associated with social media are in fact better understood as promotional work. In her study of beauty and fashion bloggers, she found that young women trying to earn money through individual online content creation (such as curating Instagram accounts, making YouTube videos or running their own blogs) were very rarely making a living from such work, and instead were dependent on various 'in kind' payments from brands, for whom they were effectively doing some paid – but more often unpaid – promotion. As Duffy shows, the precarity of these roles, combined with the aspiration of eventually 'getting paid to do what you love', meant that the women were very often losing money, while remaining 'suspended in the consumption and promotion of branded commodities' (2017: 6). More importantly, while these roles feel like 'creative' or production roles, Duffy suggests that they are more significantly promotional. Channel owners may exercise some creativity in arranging content, but recompense is strictly dependent on the success of their efforts to promote other people's brands. The struggle to reconcile their wish for fulfilling 'creative' work with the reality of promoting commercial products meant that these women spent a lot of time emphasizing their 'passion' or 'devotion' for the brands they advertised, further entrenching the promotional element of their work.

Even sectors whose main aims are educational or pedagogical may contain promotional elements in their work. In parts of the school curriculum, for example, teaching is not only concerned with the inculcation of skills and knowledge, but also with promoting particular values or attitudes. Consider the case of financial literacy education: set up with the creditable aim of ensuring that young people were aware of the dangers of debt and equipped to assess financial risk, its entry into the school curriculum was nonetheless the outcome of lobbying by groups – including banks and investment management firms – whose own interests were not neutral.[4] The approach taught in schools reflects some of this partiality. Students are encouraged (often through games and role play) to adopt an individualistic approach to financial responsibility. They are also taught to see certain forms of debt (e.g., mortgage debt) as more worthwhile than others (such as a car loan), but often without a broader understanding of *why* people might get into debt in the first place. These forms of communication promote in at least two ways: they 'move on behalf of' (i.e., advocate) a particular agenda or a set of dispositions, but they also 'move ahead of' (or anticipate) them through inculcating skills and techniques that make certain behaviours more likely. What is at stake is therefore *not* simply the transfer of information, nor 'dissemination' in Peters's (1999) sense of something relatively open, but rather purposive actions motivated by the desire to bring about a change.

A second important way in which promotional communication has become part of the fabric of work is in the apparent rise of *self*-promotion as a necessary part of working life. One of the consequences of the spread of promotional discourse is that it is now anticipated and incorporated into institutional design, incentive structures (as in the case of social media, above) and even some everyday interactions. What this means is that once a promotional modality permeates 'the micro-sphere of everyday life', it becomes increasingly difficult, or impractical, to choose *not* to be promotional subjects, since 'the penalty of not playing the game is to play it badly' (Wernick 1991: 192). In other words, the ubiquity of promotion may lead to even more promotion. Consider the following advice that political scientist Daniel Nexon offered academics in a series of tweets in June 2017 about promoting their work through social media:

> The disposition to aggressively self-promote is ... unevenly distributed ...
> But most of us don't have a choice. We need to compete for attention ...
> in an increasingly crowded info[rmation] context. (Nexon 2017; see also
> Goldhaber 2017)

Whereas in the past academics might have assumed that high-quality work would rise to the top and get noticed automatically, Nexon argued that this assumption of meritocracy is a fallacy. Thus 'the imperative of self-promotion falls on everyone who can't count on the energetic work of powerful patrons ... [so] it's well past time for mocking or belittling [those] who pay attention to, cultivate, and promote their academic brand' (Nexon 2017). But as Nexon points out, the 'fallacy of meritocracy' is due to many factors, including institutional failures that need addressing rather than simply lamenting. The sorting mechanisms for assessing quality among academics – such as journal or institutional prestige – are often both imperfect and self-reinforcing. There is, increasingly, an over-supply of qualified academics, peer review practices are poorly rewarded, and social and collegial networks continue to determine access to elite spaces. Yet while Nexon may well have been right that self-promotion is a pragmatic response to this, the problem – and the relevance for debates about promotional culture – is that self-promotion is also *itself* self-reinforcing. As Sonia Amadae (2016) notes in relation to the strategic rationality of game theory, once a strategic or instrumental rationality gets coded into the design of organizations (in the form of particular assumptions or incentive structures), it then tends to 'win out' against competing or alternative ways of doing things. Once this happens it easily takes on the appearance of merely reflecting human nature – of being evidence of the 'natural disposition every one has to persuade' asserted by Adam Smith. This, of course, leads to its further entrenchment.

Consumption and delinguistified communication

So far the examples of promotion and persuasion drawn upon in this chapter have been heavily linguistic in nature. However, a third characteristic of contemporary promotion and persuasion is that it often entails non-linguistic forms of communication. This includes product design, the design of buildings and environments, the design of services and user experiences, and the use of staged actions or events as forms of communication. These forms of persuasion are also ubiquitous, and they are often concealed or hard to identify. But their distinctive feature is that they tend to sink into the background, as taken-for-granted aspects of the environment. They often communicate in quite different registers – for example, materials, textures, fabrics, architectures – than other forms of promotion and persuasion, and taking them seriously requires thinking about media in terms of surroundings or environments (Peters 2015: 46).

One obvious example of the way such non-linguistic media function in economic life can be seen in the rise of branding (Moor 2007). The logic of branding is to find an overarching identity, set of values, or 'personality' for an organization or product, and then translate this into visual or material form. This could include standardized colours, materials and layouts, and other design features intended to capture or exemplify the brand's characteristics. The same overarching identity, personality or set of values may also be used to authorize particular behaviours or activities as consistent with the brand's identity (hence the idea that a particular activity is 'on brand'). This might mean launching new products, but also other kinds of corporate decision-making, such as how one remunerates staff.[5] Importantly, the *media* of communication produced by the logic of branding – such as uniforms, delivery vans, interior design, letter headings, and so on – are not primarily linguistic in nature (although of course written language may form part of some of these elements), but they are nonetheless all broadly strategic or promotional. And while brand identities are obviously taken into account in the production of adverts – indeed, that may be the dominant consideration – the most common forms of brand materials are more mundane, and more 'mute', in nature.

Recognition of the overlap between design and promotion (e.g., Woodham 1997; Julier 2000) has made it easier to see how much persuasion is now done in the background of other activities, through 'mute' forms of communication such as the design and curation of environments and ambiences. The philosopher Peter Sloterdijk, for example, has argued that 'the concept of product design', and 'design consciousness' more generally, were part of the operative criteria of the twentieth century (2009: 2, 9). This is because both fields make the *background environments* of human beings an explicit area to be worked upon. In much design work, as in the other examples Sloterdijk gives (including chemical warfare), the point is not to target people directly, but rather to work on the environments in which they find themselves. The interest in media as 'atmospheres' is also shared by John Durham Peters, who shows how the concepts of medium and milieu have become both 'ecological and existential' facts of nature, but also conveyances for specifically human signals and symbols (2015: 52, 48–9). A good deal of twenty-first-century promotion works in precisely this way: taking human surroundings and environments as media for meanings.

How does this modern focus on design and non-linguistic forms of promotion and persuasion play out in our economic lives? Money and personal finance are often characterized by their intangibility, but money itself is a ubiquitous, 'ambient' form of communication, which operates for the most part in a non-linguistic way. Indeed, money is the archetypal example of 'delinguistified media' given by Habermas (1987: 154–5), being a mechanism of action coordination that has been largely disconnected from discussion of norms and values. But money can also be promotional. Coins and notes, precisely through their ubiquity and mute ordinariness, may not just symbolize but also promote – in the sense of 'move in the place of' – their issuing authority. They can be examples of banal nationalism (Billig 1995). Indeed, Bourne (2017: 38) suggests that currencies are 'the quintessential state financial brand'. But they may also promote non-state financial entities too, such as the European Union in the case of the euro, or local communities that create their own alternative currencies (Moor 2018; see also chapter 2). Money in these instances may only 'promote' in the fairly weak sense of propagating or publicizing an idea or cause, but the means by which it does so exemplifies a broader tendency for promotion to operate via the materially and experientially banal.

More common than coins and cards, however, is the use of buildings and other types of infrastructure to promote particular dispositions, feelings or behaviours around economic activity. Seventeenth-century stock exchange buildings borrowed design features from Greek amphitheatres and temples (Stäheli 2008), while banks have likewise drawn strategically on classical architectural styles in order to connote stability, security and probity (Schroeder 2003). In Caitlin Zaloom's (2006) study of the Chicago Board of Trade, she shows that the design of both the building itself and the technologies housed within it was intended to 'promot[e] a relationship to the market based on observation and more explicit analysis'. At the same time as shaping activities within it, the architecture of the building had a broader symbolism and civic significance: in the case of the 1930 building, its height, bulk and adornment made it impressive, while the building's stained-glass windows showed images connecting the board and the building to forces beyond it – allegorical figures of 'Agriculture', 'Commerce' and 'Fortune' (Zaloom 2006: 27–8).

In the sphere of retail, IKEA stores are designed to configure shopping experience in a particular way. Customers must follow a set one-way path, and the layout is sufficiently 'maze-like' that backtracking, or deviating from the path, is off-putting. Knowing that it will be hard to go back later on, customers are inclined to pick up goods that attract them, and find it harder to drop them or leave them on the way to the checkout (Jansson-Boyd 2018). In the case of Apple, the layout of stores is deemed a sufficiently important part of their promotional effort that it is the subject of trademark (see Collins 2014). In both cases, physical space is designed to be strategic and communicative, but fundamentally non-discursive. This is close to what Galloway describes as a 'protocological' approach to design. A protocol is 'a technique for achieving voluntary regulation within a contingent environment' (2004: 7). This can be illustrated by the choice to put speed bumps into the road rather than change the legal speed limit: the speed bumps are more 'protocological' because they 'create a physical system of organization. They materially force the driver to acquiesce. Driving slower becomes advantageous. With bumps, the driver wants to drive more slowly … [whereas] with police presence, driving slowly can never be more than coerced behavior' (2004: 241).

As banking and commerce increasingly move online, mediated versions of this delinguistified, 'in the background' kind of promotion also appear. In Anat Balint's (2016) study of branded content on television, she recounts the case of *Overdraft Family*, an Israeli TV show about personal and household finances, and its sponsorship by Bank Hapo'alim. Regulatory restrictions forbidding direct product placement by a sponsoring brand led to more indirect efforts to communicate the brand's identity via the 'look and feel' of the programme and the locations featured. So, for example, graphics showing the family's financial information were produced using the brand's distinctive palette of colours (red and white). In later series, the programme's entire identity was modelled on the bank's brand, using red backgrounds with white lettering. A representative of the bank appeared as an adviser in the show, and meetings were held in her office, which was also organized according to the same brand guidelines. As Balint shows, the line between editorial and commercial decisions was repeatedly blurred under pressure from the sponsoring bank for deeper integration into the programme, while substantive forms of communication (in this case, discussion about household finances and debt) were often subordinated to the strategic aims of the sponsor. Yet what is perhaps most telling about this example is that from the perspective of the bank, 'product placement' was never the aim; the point was *not* to show the bank's name or logo as frequently as possible, but rather to associate the brand with the 'values' of the programme (i.e., helping people get their finances straight), and to do so in an apparently natural, seamless way – something best accomplished by this 'in the background' kind of communication.

A more recent set of developments that further underscore the extent to which design overlaps with promotion is the rise of user experience design in computing, and its specific orientation to increasing revenue. I will explore this again in the next chapter, but it refers in general to the design of computer interfaces to make them easier to navigate and more appealing to use. As Ash et al. point out, the interfaces through which users encounter digital content 'are actively designed to *modulate user action* with the aim, hope and promise of *producing desirable outcomes* for those who own and operate interfaces' (2018: 166–7, emphasis added). In this particular type of persuasive communication, design elements 'do not operate exclusively on a linguistic-representational register but involve other modulations ... such as the placement of buttons and menus, the layout of checkout pages, the colour of backgrounds and the design of sound effects and haptic feedback'. This is clearly a strategic endeavour with economic dimensions. Where websites gain their funding from advertising, content and layout are designed in such a way as to make them more 'sticky', and thus to encourage people to spend more time there (and, in turn, more likely to either view advertising content or click through onto the advertiser's page). Design is used strategically (and non-linguistically) to advance economic goals.

This strategic use of design to shape economic action can be seen in both e-commerce and financial services provision. As Joe Deville (2013) observes, lenders such as the now-defunct company Wonga draw on all kinds of 'leaky' information – including the IP addresses (and therefore rough physical location) of users, the operating systems they are using, and the route, or search terms, that may have led them to the Wonga website – in order to configure the initial 'sliders' that users are presented with when they arrive at the site. These sliders offer loan amounts and repayment periods. Although users are free to move these sliders to choose their own loan amount and repayment, Wonga's research suggests that the degree of 'slide' matters: it works as both an additional piece of data for Wonga (who have correlated magnitude of slide with likelihood of default), and as a nudge or brake on users themselves – on the basis that it is psychologically harder to make a big jump from the initial setting.

What all of these examples of strategic design communication have in common is their delinguistified quality. Although Habermas's concept of 'delinguistified media' is often associated with money itself – where it is typically used to designate systems or media that steer actors in a way that does not require communicative action, nor the consensus that emerges from it (see Heyman and Pierson 2015) – it can also be used more generally to describe mechanisms that 'uncouple action coordination from consensus formation in language' (Habermas 1987: 183). As such it has been applied to contemporary technological systems, which, in many cases, similarly steer users' behaviour without the need for communicative action, and sets limits on what can and can't be done (see, e.g., Heyman and Pierson 2015). But it can also be used more broadly to refer to forms of communication – especially strategic communication – that seek to bypass language and are thus non-interactive and non-discursive. Here I would include the branded materials and physical layouts discussed at the start of this section.

The types of delinguistified communication described here are just one particularly interesting example of a range of new forms of hiddenness that have emerged in contemporary promotional communication. Others include the rise of PR professionals, who typically work behind the scenes in order to place stories, send messages or build relationships consistent with their clients' interests (Bourne 2017). In almost all cases, PR aims to conceal its strategic aims, instead encouraging clients to lead 'public information' campaigns, or to give conference presentations and make public announcements – to engage in forms of communication that look like awareness raising, or news and information, rather than marketing and promotion (Bourne 2017). A more recent development, which shares a good deal in common with PR, is the rise of 'word of mouth' or guerrilla marketing. This entails a variety of consumer- rather than brand-generated approaches to commercial speech, often appearing in everyday or unexpected locations. As Michael Serazio notes, these forms of communication are characterized by a 'fundamental act of self-effacement' (2013: 9), in which the project of persuasion 'cloaks itself casually and even invisibly ... in an attempt to orchestrate "discovery" of the commercial message' (p. 4). Hiddenness is also central to the practice of 'astro-turfing', in which apparently grassroots movements are in fact organized and run by strategic communications firms, lobbying companies or even political parties themselves (see, e.g., Lee 2019; Waterson 2019). Finally, we might note that the rise of branded content – or native advertising – is likewise a hidden form of strategic communication that is increasingly common. Like PR, it aims to conceal its strategic purpose – often posing as a magazine feature, an advice column or a set of entertaining anecdotes or useful 'tips' for readers – and also, like PR, it is an increasingly ubiquitous part of our communications environment.

Why do these hidden and delinguistified forms of strategic communication matter? And why might they *particularly* matter for our economic lives? One part of the answer is that there is a fundamental public need for reliable information, a need that is especially acute in sectors such as personal finance, but also in our economic lives more generally. Inaccurate or misleading information has potentially serious negative consequences on wellbeing or life chances. This is especially true in the context of 'infoglut' (Andrejevic 2013), where suspicions of partiality and 'interestedness' are rife and where there may be a tendency to short-circuit difficult decisions precisely because of the difficulty of judging credibility amid a flood of confusing or incompatible messages. But there is also another reason, which has to do with the public's right to know the source of the information and messages they receive. This 'right to know' is not a constitutional right but is often at the heart of freedom of information legislation as well as various forms of consumer protection (Schudson 2015). Those advancing the cause have made different arguments on its behalf: in the case of consumer information, one argument is that consumers need to be able to make 'rational comparisons' of price in order for a market economy to function properly; another (made by John F. Kennedy) is that markets have become so impersonal and abstract, and so dominated by 'mass advertising ... [and] arts of persuasion' (cited in Schudson 2015: 67), that the environment itself has changed. The market is no longer a place of 'store owners or employees hoping to maintain a relationship with a repeat customer', but a place where commodities and brands try to seduce consumers by any means. Ideally, the public would also be able to know, or at least infer, the intentions behind the messages. Frank Pasquale (2015) has pointed out that there is an increasing incongruity between what corporations are able to know about ordinary people compared to what ordinary people are able to know about them (matched by a corresponding ability of the powerful to keep secrets, while ordinary people are able to keep fewer and fewer). Fighting for a 'right to know' something about the origin and intention of messages is here part of a larger struggle to correct this growing asymmetry.

And what about the delinguistified nature of much strategic communication? There may not be much that we can do about banks' desires to use classical motifs to connote stability or brands' desire to express their 'personality' through particular fabrics and colours. Nonetheless, it is important to bear in mind that any attempt to uncover, challenge or dispute promotional efforts aimed at us will usually require language and dialogue. Moreover, while some kinds of delinguistified communication seem relatively benign, there are others – for example in the selling of consumer credit or the pricing of goods – where hiddenness and silence may be much more consequential. Hidden strategic communication is never good for the public sphere, but even concealed promotion can potentially be disputed if it relies on words – a 'puff piece' in a newspaper can be uncovered, or its contents disputed (see, e.g., Plunkett and Quinn 2015). The newer challenge is that many contemporary forms of strategic communication are wordless, and their mechanism of action is hidden. Power is then inscribed across our economic lives in ways that are much harder to challenge or even name.

Conclusion

For much of the twentieth and early twenty-first centuries, it was fairly easy to identify advertising and other types of promotional communication. During this time, as Michael Serazio (2013) puts it, 'we knew what advertising looked like and we knew where to find it: during the programming break on TV, surrounding the editorial content in a newspaper, or across banners atop a web page'. This remains true, to a greater or lesser extent, of many contemporary forms of promotion: endless marketing emails, or advertisements in our social media feeds, are easy to identify and for the most part easy to delete or ignore. We have developed the ability to identify and 'frame' messages and interactions according to certain criteria, and this is helped by the fact that most forms of communication also include meta-communicative messages that announce their purpose. We may dislike the content of these advertising messages, and there may be good reasons to try to limit the amount of such material in our lives, but they have the advantage of not concealing their strategic intention and this makes interpretation easier.

In this chapter, however, I have claimed that such readily identifiable marketing messages are only one part of the way that promotional communication constructs our economic lives, and that strategic or self-advancing communication is far more ubiquitous than we often believe. Promotional speech does not always announce itself clearly, not least because it is so closely intertwined with other forms of speech. The first part of the chapter pointed to the ways in which the language used to describe the economy – by economists, central bankers or politicians, for example – can be promotional, in the sense of being interested, often self-advancing, and aiming to move others to action or belief. The second part of the chapter showed how promotional communication has become a core part of a range of jobs that are not ostensibly part of the marketing industries; from retailing to teaching to social media content producing, far more jobs than we would imagine have a strategic and persuasive quality at their heart. The chapter also explored the case of *self*-promotion, and showed that in many sectors, the perceived need to self-promote can be traced to various institutional failings that mean conventional paths to recognition are no longer felt to be viable. Here I argued that the logic of self-promotion is entirely self-reinforcing: in a world in which everyone is engaged in self-promotion, it becomes costly *not* to join in, and this in turn reinforces the sense that such activity is part of a natural human instinct, rather than a response to a particular set of institutional or social cues.

The final part of the chapter returned to the sphere of consumption with which promotion is most typically associated, but focused on a form of promotion that has historically received less attention than advertising or PR. This is what I term (following Habermas) 'delinguistified' promotional communication: communication that is not primarily linguistic and that relies instead on the use of colour, shape, layout and material to prompt association and meaning-making on the part of users or audiences. This type of communication also seeks to persuade and is more widespread than we might first assume. The most prominent instance of this type of communication is probably branding, a practice that takes materials, objects and environments as communications media, and then uses them to wordlessly create associations or feelings in the mind of consumers. However, its logic is continuous with what Sloterdijk (2009) has described as the twentieth-century urge to target people's environments, and to make these an object of explicit reflection and calculation. The extent to which design is therefore the organizing principle of delinguistified communication was illustrated by a final example, of computer interfaces whose intention is to achieve certain strategic ends, whether encouraging users to stay on the site longer, or to reveal more information, or to make particular economic decisions and choices.

What all of the aspects of economic life covered in this chapter have in common is that they are sites where promotional or persuasive communication is blurred together with other types of utterance. Indeed, what I have been trying to suggest is that promotional or persuasive communication is rarely a 'pure' form – advertisements are in this sense exceptions, or limit cases – and that this is part of what makes it such a ubiquitous area of our economic lives. There is, as I have indicated, a growing tendency to hide promotional communication (e.g., by dressing it up as 'word of mouth', or branded content, or well-disguised PR). But it is also true that a good deal of persuasive communication is 'hidden' for the simple reason that it is bound together with other types of economic communication such as describing, informing or teaching.

How much does the hiddenness of promotional communication matter? There are good reasons to ensure that people are aware of the difference between promotional and informational communications. If ostensibly informational or even educational communications are shot through with promotional elements, the work of interpretation becomes more difficult with potentially meaningful economic consequences. We might also argue that we have a fundamental *right* to know both when we are being targeted by promotional speech, and where such messages originate (Schudson 2015). One argument, which combines the philosophical with the pragmatic, is that if we cannot be sure whether we are being targeted by commercial messages or not, and if we are not aware of how we are being classified or 'placed' by those hidden messages, this will lead to envy and suspicion in the public sphere (Turow 2006), with serious consequences for public trust and for the future of markets as any kind of shared space.

These kinds of questions have taken on greater urgency with the rise of algorithms and software that work 'behind the scenes' of user experience to promote particular actions or to channel behaviour in particular directions. Here the question of 'delinguistified' media becomes directly relevant: it is not just that these media do not *require* communicative action; it is that in many cases they actively discourage or inhibit it. In bypassing linguistic processes of deliberation or consensus formation, delinguistified media are therefore explicitly anti-political. Indeed, the rise of hidden strategic communications, the blurring of promotional with other types of speech, and the stifling of debate or contestation through delinguistified media would all seem to require a response focused on rendering the invisible visible (Deville and van der Velden 2016), or making the implicit explicit. Perhaps the advance of self-advancing or deceptive promotion can be halted by a new emphasis on information. With this in mind, it is to the question of information in economic life – its circulation, qualities and limits – that I turn in the next chapter.

Chapter 4

Information

This chapter focuses on a type of communicative action long understood to be central to economic life. The plentiful supply and availability of information is considered, alongside competition, to be one of two prerequisites for an efficiently functioning market. As a type of utterance, informing tends to have a more open quality than the cases of promoting and persuading described in the last chapter; it has more to do with a logic of *dissemination*, in which one is free to respond to messages as one wishes, or not at all (Peters 1999). Informing, at least in theory, is not motivated by the desire to change, and thus may be seen as less coercive than many other types of communication. Partly for this reason, information is often seen as the currency of democratic societies, many of which formalize this through principles of the 'right to know' or some kind of freedom of information legislation (Schudson 2015). And yet many critical communication scholars find the concept of information to be tainted. The development of information *theory* over the course of the twentieth century meant purging it of both its embodied qualities and its connection to semantics or meaning (Hayles 1999). And as we saw in chapter 1, scholars like Carey (1997 [1994]) thought 'information' was simply an economist's term for what was left once all of the communal or political qualities of 'communication' had been removed.

This chapter explores some of these ambivalences of information as they shape an economy increasingly interwoven with digital media and technologies. Digital media were, by many accounts, supposed to set information free, releasing it from the concentration and institutional control of previous eras, and unleashing new waves of both democracy and free trade. While this chapter cannot explore the fate of political speech, it does consider the sometimes-contradictory ways in which the circulation of information constructs economic life. While it is true that digital media make new volumes of information available, and that this produces both new types of exchange and new pools of information around existing ones, it is also the case that much economic activity now depends on either collecting people's data in ways they are barely aware of, trading in it, or restricting access to information for reasons of commercial advancement (Pasquale 2015). There is a good deal of information inequality – or information asymmetry – in this situation, which has significant social and economic implications, and with which regulators have been slow to catch up. These developments also remind us that 'informing' can have two distinct senses – one which is more open and has to do with providing people with useful facts or descriptions, but another which is more secretive and has to do with passing valuable, even incriminating, information to authorities.

The chapter begins by outlining what many would see as the more positive consequences of information abundance: the introduction of new volumes of information into routine exchanges, and the creation of new types of economic action and opportunity. As we will see, however, these advantages can easily shade into disadvantages: the efficiency gains of many platform-based systems can be outweighed by their anti-competitive tendencies and unfair labour practices, and the advantages to consumers of greater volumes of information can easily shade into information overload and lack of trust in the origin and credibility of information. I then turn to explore the nature of these information problems in greater detail: specifically, the fact that more information is now produced *about* consumers – and, increasingly, employees and workers – often behind their backs, and stored in ways that are inaccessible to them. I consider the use of such data in workplace productivity tools, in cases of 'marketing discrimination' (Turow 2011), as well as in contemporary price personalization and price discrimination techniques. I conclude the chapter by considering whether 'informing' is really as benign and non-coercive a form of communication as it first seems.

New volumes of information

The capacity to produce new types and volumes of information is a key characteristic of online economies, and of the digital infrastructures that underpin contemporary exchange. Historically, inadequate or asymmetrical information has been understood to pose a problem for the efficient functioning of markets, and it was correspondingly thought that 'irrational' behaviour could be ameliorated, at least in part, through fuller information (see, e.g., Akerlof 1970; Fourcade and Healy 2017). Digital technologies promise to improve this situation, as a result of the sheer ease with which high volumes of information can be produced and shared. However, this ease of production has varied consequences: on the one hand, it is easier for consumers to find information about companies, products, contracts and so on, and to share information in ways that strengthen their position; at the same time, there may be too much information to process, its credibility may be hard to assess, or the means to do so may lie in the hands of companies rather than consumers (Andrejevic 2013). Furthermore, new volumes of information are now automatically produced *about* consumers as a by-product of their routine actions, and often without their knowledge. The use and sharing of such information are often matters of some secrecy, even while such information is also an object of monetization and commodification. This produces a complicated picture of the informational ecology of online economies.

Reviews and ratings, for example, are one obvious way in which communication among consumers supports economic activity. In reviewing products, customers provide each other with information about goods and services, but they also express opinions, present themselves and 'talk back' to companies. These forms of communication are useful to both companies and consumers. Information increases efficiency by reducing consumers' search costs, but it is also good for companies by alerting them to potential problems in a timely fashion. Some companies provide 'pre-structured' feedback systems on shopping sites; elsewhere the space for reviews is more open. Bulletin boards or other discussion forums may be embedded in the site: auction site eBay contains significant conversational features that not only make up for gaps in information in the sense that economists would recognize (see Kollock 1999) but also 'personalize' exchange in a way that sociologists or anthropologists would acknowledge. Such informational and conversational opportunities are so central to markets that they can even be observed in so-called 'darknet' markets for drugs and other illicit goods, either through in-built opportunities to leave reviews or through consumer discussion elsewhere (Sutcliffe 2017). However, as we shall see below, while these forms of rating by consumers are public and visible, the rating of consumers by companies is, for the most part, private.

Many developments in information sharing dramatically enhance the capacity of customers to express themselves through 'voice', rather than the traditionally preferred option of 'exit' (Hirschman 1970; see also chapter 1). While voice is often seen as a 'messier' form of information than exit, it also clearly provides more helpful and fine-grained information for those companies that are able to read and interpret it. Voice can also be seen in another area of contemporary digital economies, that is, the growth of advice and discussion forums. While some of these forums are explicitly oriented towards people's economic lives, others discuss issues of money, finance and consumption in the context of some other issue, such as parenting or relationships. What makes these forums interesting is that they are much more autonomous than the reviewing or rating opportunities embedded in e-commerce sites. They offer a space in which economic practices can be discussed and questioned at some length, over a sustained period of time, and in which new norms can emerge (see Moor and Kanji 2019). They also offer a space in which, to use Latour's (2004) phrase, matters of fact may become matters of concern – even matters of controversy and politics. A number of studies have followed such sites and traced how discussion, debate, information seeking and the provision of mutual support sometimes evolve into more structured forms of politicization. Gambles (2010) shows that debates on the website Mumsnet produce both 'personal publics' (public discussions rooted in personal experience and 'lay expertise') and 'political publics' – spaces that are points of reference for politicians (who have been keen to court vocal and well-educated Mumsnet users) but also spaces for political mobilization and lobbying around issues of concern to users. Similarly, in the case of discussion forums about debt, Deville (2016) shows how an apparently private, isolating and even shameful experience can be transformed into one in which one feels part of a collectivity, even a 'public'. They do this by offering information, advice and moral support, and by activities (such as 'unmasking' typical creditor tactics, or copying and pasting private letters for everyone to read) that turn critical scrutiny back onto the behaviour of creditors rather than debtors. As Deville points out, over time these conversations and discussions coalesce into a 'complex, messy public archive', which is not only available to users but to anyone searching for information online. I consider these forms of discussion again in chapter 6.

As these studies indicate, the internet offers considerable scope for people to inform themselves about matters relating to their economic lives that might traditionally have been considered 'private', or restricted to conversations with close friends, and to share this with a much wider audience. Issues related to money, debt and household finances are prime contenders for such treatment, and there are many such spaces online. One of the advantages of such sites is that they are typically anonymous and separate from the concerns of corporate owners. Another is that discussion is not restricted (as it usually is on e-commerce sites) to specific products or services, but can range much more widely, from tips about supermarket discounts to entire livelihood strategies. In this way, they capture the more values-driven (i.e., sociological) understanding of economic life outlined at the start of this book, in which 'economic' concerns are entwined with other non-economic areas of life, including debates about politics, family, morality, and so on. These forms of economic communication are, for many people, much more important to their economic lives than news reports about industrial change or central bank inflation forecasts.

These information-sharing sites and infrastructures are some of the most positive developments associated with the impact of the internet on people's economic lives. They may be construed, following Preda (2009: 97) as a type of amateur 'information group' – that is, a group situated 'outside' the market that can produce, disseminate and process information about it. Other examples of this might include DIY or non-professional investment sites, which some say have led to a diminishing of the power of corporate PR practitioners to dominate discussion of companies' value (Bourne 2017). Some online groups and forums may acquire their own lobbying power: Money Saving Expert and The Big Deal, for example, negotiate price deals with companies because they are of sufficient size to offer a credible and attractive set of new customers. In other cases, what they offer is more like a community: a form of peer support and advice that sometimes leads to political mobilization. Even when they do not do this, they still provide people with support in decision-making, and demystify the activities of more powerful economic actors. In this way they can offset some of the losses associated with the decline of face-to-face contact in economic life.

New forms of exchange and new economic models

The same communications technologies that facilitate the injection of greater volumes of information into and around moments of exchange have also started to facilitate new types and volumes of exchange, often between people located at great physical distances from one another. Indeed, from an economic perspective, online trade has the potential to reduce entry barriers and some of the transaction costs associated with running a business. This should potentially allow people without large reserves of money to enter markets, and without many of the traditional costs associated with starting a small enterprise. It also allows people to create additional revenue streams for themselves, and to diversify their economic activities in relatively low-cost ways (Coyle 2016).

One important characteristic of digitally facilitated trade – particularly business to consumer trade – is that it increasingly involves platforms of various kinds. While much online exchange is still organized around a conventional buyer–seller relationship, a growing number of online businesses are structured around a central intermediary who 'matches' buyers and sellers, and takes a cut of sales that follow. This is especially clear in the case of platforms like Uber, Airbnb, Etsy, Depop and others. Some platforms may make most of their money from advertising and the sale of user data, but if the platform's main purpose is economic exchange, then profits typically come from payments and fees associated with online transactions. In fact, these platform businesses are often commodified versions of sites that offered comparable but non-monetized forms of exchange, such as couchsurfing.com, originally a community-oriented platform that offered places to stay to a network of like-minded users. What has changed, through commodification, is their scale and reach.

While critics point to the rentier-like nature of such platforms in making most of their profits by extracting fees, economists point to their advantages in smoothing market frictions (Evans and Schmalensee 2016). Platforms, but in fact e-commerce in general, can enhance competition because with a greater range of suppliers to choose from, goods and services are likely to be available at a wider range of price points, allowing more people to participate and to find items they want at a price they can afford. There is an associated gain in terms of efficiency. Digital platforms typically allow for the better coordination of supply and demand, and therefore a reduction of inefficiency and waste. In some cases, such as eBay or Freecycle, this coordination also entails greater reuse and recycling of goods, and thus has further advantages in terms of environmental efficiency and the conservation of natural resources (Coyle 2016).

And yet the new exchange systems are vulnerable to specific types of problems. Many of these 'multi-sided' platforms are characterized by direct or indirect network effects, in which value can be created for both sides (and for platform owners) by bringing lots of people together, but which also require careful management in order to balance the often-conflicting interests of the different parties. While economists have spent some time considering the particular pricing structures that might achieve such a balance (Rochet and Tirole 2003; Evans and Schmalensee 2016), the issues for consumers are somewhat different. As anyone who has joined a large social media platform knows, once a network reaches a certain size it can be hard to leave, even if one is dissatisfied. In the case of social media, this 'lock-in' comes from the fact that it feels less like a product than an integral part of one's social world, something that satisfies human needs for 'self-expression, voice, influence … empowerment, and connection'

(Zuboff 2015: 79) and is not easily given up. But lock-in also comes from the fact that there may be few alternatives; once a network has reached a certain size, most potential users migrate to that platform. The difficulty of 'exit' because of a lack of competing alternatives means that platforms – for example a ride-sharing network such as Uber – can then raise their prices, or change terms and conditions, with few consequences. This is one reason why questions about competition and antitrust come up so frequently with regard to platforms (see Economist 2016; Coyle 2017).

While the infrastructure of such forms of exchange is oriented to action and intervention in the world, rather than personal expression (Fuller and Goffey 2012), they do nonetheless enable and in some cases rely on information and communication. The ranking and rating of goods and services on e-commerce sites, as well as the ranking of people by each other and as part of platform-based transactions such as those on Uber and Airbnb, seems on the surface to perform the classic role of a trust mechanism. Reviews, as I have outlined above, fill in informational gaps, allowing people to feel more confident in making a purchase. To the extent that the owner of, for example, a hotel or Airbnb property can interact directly with individual customers, we may even speak of a 're-personalization' of exchange, in the sense of exchanges coming to absorb more and more information about persons (Hart 2001: 322). On the other hand, the ubiquity of rating and ranking, and their often-self-interested nature, may also create suspicion about the origin and trustworthiness of information. There have been a number of cases of 'fake' reviews on sites such as Trip Advisor (Bradshaw 2012) and Amazon (Smithers 2019). Fake comments and ratings are alleged to be common on Chinese e-commerce sites (Yang 2018), and Amazon only put a stop to 'incentivized' reviews – in which consumers were offered free or discounted goods in exchange for reviews – in 2016. In cases like this, rather than enhancing information, digital technologies may simply create a new set of information problems for markets to deal with. They also create strong incentives for strategic behaviour on both sides – sometimes in ways that are beneficial, but sometimes not. Uber's two-way reviewing system, for example, may be good if it makes customers more courteous and respectful, or makes cab owners drive more carefully. But it can also create suspicion, stoke fears of manipulated information, and make people worry about how they have been judged.

Another way in which information technologies and infrastructures are producing new forms of economic activity is in their capacity to intervene in the production and circulation of money itself. The impact of changes in computing infrastructure on flows of economic information is a key element of the rise of alternative and cryptocurrencies, and the structures of knowledge and verification that accompany them. These new currencies – from high-profile cryptocurrencies such as Bitcoin to local digital currencies such as the Liverpool Pound – also speak to another key theme of this chapter: that is, the tension between the potential for greater 'personalization' on the one hand, and issues of privacy and surveillance on the other. As part of this, they are also bound up with the related issue of who controls information about economic transactions, and who, if anyone, can profit from it.

What cryptocurrencies share with local currencies and local exchange trading schemes (LETS) is a belief that the interests of powerful institutions such as national banks and global corporations are not necessarily aligned with those of ordinary people. On the other hand, the original aims of cryptocurrencies typically had less to do with community and financial inclusion than with resistance to state and corporate surveillance, and to the ability of payment intermediaries (such as PayPal) to extract profits – and monetizable data – from basic financial transactions (Maurer et al. 2013: 265; see also chapter 2). The original goal of Bitcoin was to find a means of transacting with others that did not involve either scrutiny by unaccountable corporate intermediaries, or being 'taxed' by them in the form of unreasonably high fees. It emerged, in other words, out of a lack of trust in the existing infrastructure and the belief that it was possible to build a better one. Bitcoin's alternative – a 'distributed ledger' system, which kept transactions public but anonymous, and authenticated them through a collective form of verification incentivized by the right to mine new 'coins' – did not so much involve trust in an alternative community, but rather as Maurer et al. (2013) point out, dispensed with the need to trust 'anyone but the code'. While it may have succeeded in avoiding oversight by powerful third parties, its own system 'begin[s] from the assumption that there is no trust and no community, only individual economic agents acting in self-interest' (O'Dwyer 2015).

Bitcoin has fallen out of favour with progressives for a number of reasons. The computing power required to solve the (increasingly difficult) cryptographic puzzles attached to 'blocks' of transactions – which leads to the right to mine new coins – is now so great that it excludes all but large groups and those with the money to buy and run the latest super-computers. This leads to a *social* distribution within the system that is deeply at odds with the horizontal logic initially imagined. In addition, serious security loopholes have been found, so its feted security and fraud protections are not what they seemed; for this reason, many early adopters of Bitcoin have migrated to other currencies with better security credentials. Thirdly, users of cryptocurrencies increasingly treat them as a speculative asset (i.e., a store of value) rather than a means of payment, so the initial aim of challenging the excesses of 'flow capitalists' has been subordinated to its function as a highly speculative form of investment – what some have called a 'Ponzi scheme for libertarians' (O'Brien 2015). Indeed, the fact that its value is so unstable is one of the reasons why its potential as a means of payment may not be achieved. Finally, the broader culture of Bitcoin has been challenged: both its 'right-wing extremism' (Golumbia 2016), and the apparently masculinist sensibility linked to the combination of anarchism and libertarianism that underpins much crypto-currency development (see also O'Dwyer 2015).

Bitcoin's significance is increasingly believed to lie less in the system itself than in the innovations of blockchain technology – that is, the distributed public ledger system for verifying transactions and avoiding fraud. This has appeal both to progressives and capitalists. As Bollier (2015) points out, it solves a 'vexing collective action problem' in a network context by helping to assure the authenticity of things transacted (coins, documents, identities, votes, etc.), but it also has the potential to enable new forms of community governance – specifically, to spread non-hierar-chical ways of organizing in which 'intelligence is spread on the edges of the network instead of being concentrated at the center' (de Filippi cited in Bollier 2015). This is a quite different way of organizing information than the one we can observe in 'mainstream' economic activity, as I will describe in the next sections.

The development of blockchain technology in new contexts will pose a number of questions about economic communication. The advantages of blockchain have come to be seen (by state and commercial actors at least) primarily in terms of its security and fraud preventing capabilities, but it is worth remembering that its roots also lie in the effort to avoid surveillance by powerful institutions – to guarantee individual anonymity, even while making records of transactions shared. It is not clear whether future uses of blockchain technology will preserve this. Proposed future uses have included – to name just a few – inter-bank transfers (Detrixhe and Wong 2017), the distribution of grants in higher education (Wong 2016) and welfare payments. In some cases, the point is precisely *not* just to ensure secure transmission and storage but also to keep track of how, when and by whom money is spent. Indeed, one of the criticisms of a trial involving paying welfare allowances with blockchain technology was that it had the potential to allow governments to observe how recipients were spending their money, and, in the future, to place limits on where they could spend it or how much they could spend (Cellan-Jones 2016). The UK government Chief Scientific Adviser published a report in 2016 suggesting that government should back trials of blockchain technology because of its potential 'to help governments to collect taxes, deliver benefits, issue passports, record land registries, assure the supply chain of goods and generally ensure the integrity of government records and services'. At the same time, he noted, the technology 'offers the potential, *according to the circumstances*, for individual consumers to control access to personal records and know who has accessed them' (Walport 2016: 6, emphasis added)

Software, algorithms and proprietary data

The production of new types and volumes of information online clearly has ambivalent consequences. The biggest issue, from the perspective of consumers – but also, increasingly, employees – is the production and harvesting of data about them in ways they may be only barely aware of. This is ubiquitous online, and increasingly done automatically or semi-automatically. Data mining accompanies almost every action on websites; as Robert Gehl notes, in Web 2.0 '[site owners] seek to surveil every action, store the resulting data, protect that data via intellectual property, and mine it for profit' (Gehl 2011: 1228). The same is true for social media communications and in both cases the link between communication, information and monetary exchange is extremely tight. In very many cases, human actions online are mined to produce information that is easily suited to customization for advertising, whether by the site itself or third-party advertisers (Turow 2011). Indeed, the very architecture of sites – particularly platforms like Facebook – is often designed to encourage forms of behaviour that both create valuable data and at the same time loop others into that architecture, producing information not just about actions, preferences and pathways but about patterns of relationship over time. Certain sites, in other words, have a vested commercial interest in 'promoting' communication and interaction, for the purposes of creating and selling information.

Developments such as these have led some to suggest that human communications online are increasingly just 'the tip of a huge pyramid of data flows, *most of which occur between machines*' (Hayles cited in Beer 2009: 988, emphasis added). In this context, an increasing number of decisions are made without human agency, even while humans may set their parameters. This tension between the potential of digital technology to produce new volumes of information *for* consumers, including new opportunities to discuss economic matters, and its potential to extract large amounts of information *from* individuals, often without their knowing, is itself underpinned by developments in digital architecture and infrastructure. Of course, communications infrastructures have always played a role in determining flows of information, people and goods – this is as true of roads, railways and cables as it is of the architecture of specific websites or platforms (Innis 1950; Peters 2015). In Zaloom's (2006) work on the Chicago Board of Trade, for example, the infrastructure and layout of the building is essential for flows of information 'about' the market, something that was true long before the advent of digitalization.

Nonetheless, while an attentive observer such as Zaloom might be able to show how the design and layout of a building shapes the flows of people and information within it, the architecture and infrastructures of the digital age are notably hard to observe. Indeed, the declining visibility of infrastructures that shape our economic lives is a recurring concern in recent work (Galloway 2004; Hayles 2006; Pasquale 2015). What is at stake is that while more and more data than ever before is generated, the means to store and sort that data is increasingly hidden from view and concentrated in the hands of a relatively small number of intermediaries who know how to interpret and deploy it (see Andrejevic 2013; Pasquale 2015). And while this invisible infrastructure of data processing has consequences for specific *kinds* of economic activity, as we shall see below, there is also a broader claim to consider, namely that communications infrastructures are becoming so closely tied to commercial activity that 'it is rather hard to identify times when we are *not* in a marketplace' (Zinkham cited in McGuigan and Manzerolle 2015: 1838). More and more online activity – even apparently non-commercial activity – is one way or another geared towards the collection of information that can be used for marketing in the future.

It is worth noting that while much of this data collection is associated with e-commerce sites, or with tracking consumers across the web in ways that can ultimately be used for marketing, this is not the only way that data collection shapes our economic lives. There is now considerable evidence that the same practices are being extended to our roles as workers. What some have called the 'datafication' of employment (Adler-Bell and Miller 2018) extends from the very beginning of the hiring process – including the way that job ads are targeted so that only certain people see them

– through to the selection process, employee monitoring once people are in post, performance evaluation and forecasting, and even redundancy (see Sanchez-Monedero and Dencik 2019).

While this 'algorithmic management' can be performed through specialist applications and platforms that companies buy as 'extras' to support particular tasks (such as advertising or hiring), it is also embedded into software such as Microsoft 365, which many employees must use as a routine part of their work. Microsoft was criticised in late 2020 for introducing a range of new metrics into 365, which technology researcher Wolfie Christl (2020) showed could analyse employees' behaviours at the individual level, including 'the number of days an employee has been sending emails, using the chat, using "mentions" in email, etc'. It also offered companies the facility to combine these into a 'Microsoft Productivity Score', which, Christl suggested, turned the system into a 'full-fledged workplace surveillance tool'. Many of these features were scaled back in response to criticism, but Microsoft still collects lots of data that can be used to 'inform' on workers. Its Teams remote working and communication platform collects three types of data about users, including census data, which means data about device, language and operating system, and error reporting data, but also usage data. This includes the number of messages sent and the number of calls and meetings joined (Stokel-Walker 2020). It also gathers profile data, including the content of meetings, shared files and transcripts, all of which can be stored for 30 days.

If information abundance is the defining characteristic of our age, then its ownership and the means for storing and sorting it are inevitably the most critical questions. The means for storing large volumes of data is usually the privately owned database, and the way in which something meaningful or useful is extracted from it is, increasingly, the proprietary algorithm or other analytic technique. Algorithms, in essence, are 'encoded procedures for transforming input data into a desired output, based on specified calculations' (Gillespie 2014: 1); their task is to select what is most *relevant* from a corpus of data for a particular purpose. Relevance is a contested concept, but while algorithmic operations on data have sometimes been compared to the role of human editors on newspapers (Gillespie 2014; Tufekci 2015), one of the chief attractions of algorithmic data sorting is in fact that it promises to overcome human error or subjective bias (Pasquale 2015; Fourcade and Healy 2017). This is an important claim in areas such as credit scoring and loan decisions, which have historically been based on bias, whim and prejudice (Pasquale 2015: 102). But the promise of algorithmic objectivity may be misleading:

the assumption that 'a machine-driven, software-enabled system is going to offer better results than human judgment' is itself a kind of bias (MacKenzie quoted in Pasquale 2015: 107), and algorithms still have to establish legitimacy in their claims to 'jurisdiction over the ability to objectively parse reality' (Schudson and Anderson cited in Gillespie 2014: 181).

This lack of legitimacy has been demonstrated by a number of studies that have found evidence of 'algorithmic bias' and racism. In a case described by Safiya Umoja Noble (2018), a Black-owned hairdressing business in the United States found it almost impossible to attract customers on the review platform Yelp because the algorithm used to match consumer search terms with business listings did not recognize the search term 'Black hair' as meaningful. As Kandis, the business owner, puts it:

> You are telling us we have to use certain keywords, and you don't even know our language, because you think that 'Black hair' means hair *color*, not hair *texture*! We don't call each other African American; society calls us that. Do you know what I mean? We are Black. (cited in Noble 2018: 177, emphasis in original)

In this case, Kandis is well aware that her relative invisibility on the site reflects both the biases of predominantly white engineers, who cannot anticipate the search term 'Black hair', and the biases of Yelp itself, whose priority is to extract as much money from her in order to make her profile more visible. Elsewhere, the main source of algorithmic bias is input data. An investigation by ProPublica in 2017 showed that Facebook allowed advertisers to use anti-Semitic categories to target users, because those categories – including 'Jew hater' and 'how to burn Jews' – were automatically (i.e., algorithmically) generated based on 'what users explicitly share with Facebook and what they implicitly convey through their online activity' (Angwin et al. 2017). While Facebook subsequently removed those categories, its advertising platform is based on an algorithm that 'automatically transforms people's declared interests into advertising categories'. In a previous study, ProPublica had found that Facebook allowed its advertisers to prevent adverts being shown to groups including African-Americans, Hispanics and Asian-Americans (Angwin and Parris 2016).

Marketing discrimination

As the above examples show, one of the main uses of algorithmic sorting techniques is for marketing and promotion. Marketers regularly generate customer profiles so that marketing messages can be more carefully targeted, but more sophisticated examples of this can be found in the 'recommendation algorithms' of companies like Amazon and Spotify, although the automated sorting of customers means that even the most routine marketing messages will try to identify gender, types of past purchases, and so on. Concerns that this profiling and targeting of content – whether for marketing or some other purpose – will create 'filter bubbles' have existed for some time (Sunstein 2001; Pariser 2011). These concerns typically focus on access to news content, given the implications for democratic participation of a citizenry that shares no common sense of the issues of the day and disagrees about basic facts (Turow 2006; Tufekci 2015). This has particular relevance for debates about economic learning and understanding and news coverage of the economy outlined in previous chapters: put bluntly, if algorithms offer news stories to readers based on their past preferences, people who do not read economic news because it is too difficult to understand (or too boring) will get less and less of it in the future, reinforcing their exclusion from public debate on those topics. That exclusion from economic discourse may have its roots in decisions by governments about what to teach at school, or decisions by editors about how much contextual information to provide about economic news, but it is certainly reinforced and exacerbated by algorithmic filtering.

These concerns have spread to more obviously 'cultural' content too, and recently scholars have expressed particular worries about the ways that data collection and algorithmic sorting are used to produce 'carefully designed customer categories – or niches – that tag consumers as desirable or undesirable for their business' (Turow cited in Beer 2009: 990). This includes making inferences about their wealth or potential value to the company, based on such things as the mobile device or computer operating system they are using, but also their previous spending history with a particular company, or many other things (Moor and Lury 2018). This may have direct consequences for how customers are treated: in cases where companies can identify a user and their purchase history by their phone number or email address, algorithms can be used to offer different service experiences and, in principle, to prioritize the experiences of more valuable or more loyal customers. Such sorting tends to occur in a way that is automated and mostly invisible, such that 'neither the losers nor the beneficiaries are even aware that they are in operation' (Graham cited in Beer 2009: 990).

For many authors, what is at stake in such developments is a new form of social profiling and discrimination. According to Joseph Turow,

for example, 'marketing discrimination' matters because the advertisements offered to people are a kind of status signal: 'they alert people as
to their social position' and 'if you consistently get ads for low-priced
cars ... fast-food restaurants and other products that reflect a lower-class
status, your sense of the world's opportunities may be narrower than that
of someone who is feted with ads for ... international trips and luxury
products' (2011: 6). Similarly, for Fourcade and Healy (2017: 23), differen-
tiated marketing – 'targeting individuals according to the likelihood that
they will be more or less receptive to particular kinds of products or ideas'
– is problematic in part because it 'presupposes a relatively immobile social
order or set preferences, and may end up deepening those differences by
reinforcing the behaviors that caused them to be identified in the first
place'.

In fact, advertising has targeted people according to presumptions about
their social position since long before the existence of the internet, or
algorithmic forms of data sorting. And poorer people are sent messages
about their social status – including the regard (or disregard) in which
they are held by the wealthy – all the time, and across many spheres; it
is not obvious why marketing messages should be uniquely powerful in
this regard, or especially likely to shape self-image and perceptions of
'the world's opportunities'. Indeed, to make this claim one would have
to ignore all the ways in which the poor are made aware of their subor-
dinate status in school, at work, in relations with the state, and so on.
Nor is it clear that digitally targeted marketing online is any more likely
to 'act back' on people's practices and behaviours than an advert in the
newspaper you read, or the television shows you watch. As anyone who
has received a targeted ad knows, the most effective ads are usually those
showing products you have already found for yourself (i.e., things you
were already planning to buy), while the potential for misrecognition is
very large. More specialist areas may be more effective in this kind of
targeting – the Amazon and Spotify recommendation algorithms are
notably successful in introducing people to new content, for example – but
even here there is still a danger of falling for the 'myth of the mediated
centre' (Couldry 2006) where we assume that media 'direct' things, and
ignore all of the other social, educational or institutional processes at work
in the formation of tastes and choices.

We should not ignore the implications of the fact that more and more
of the media content we encounter is curated or pre-structured for
us in advance, but the argument I want to make here is that the more
serious and consequential aspects of marketing classifications, from the

perspective of how our economic lives are mediated, are in fact their connection to other scores and rankings that *directly* determine access to certain goods and services, and the price at which they can be accessed. Credit scores – as Fourcade and Healy (2017) note – are uniquely powerful in this regard, since they are used to decide whether certain categories of goods (e.g., mortgages) are accessible at all, as well as to develop segmented pricing strategies by which 'riskier' individuals are asked to pay more – often much more – for certain kinds of borrowing. More worryingly, credit scores are also increasingly used 'off label' (Rona-Tas 2017) in a range of contexts that have nothing to do with offering credit, including by landlords in selecting tenants, and even in company hiring decisions. If such practices are allowed to continue, these elements of marketing discrimination are likely to be far more consequential for our economic lives than taste-based recommendations and advertisements.

Price personalization

At the cutting edge of these marketing discrimination practices is the ability to 'personalize' or 'customize' the prices offered to people on the basis of fine-grained, automatically collected and regularly updated data. This data may not just be about consumers themselves, but can be linked to aspects of their environment, such as weather and season, or to shifting levels of supply and demand. Increasingly, many different kinds of data can be included in generating and presenting a single price, and this has consequences both for how price is experienced – it is more fluid and fast-moving than it was in much of the recent past – and for how it is used to distinguish between, and act on, different consumers. As part of these developments, price's communicative role – which I outlined in chapter 2 – is also changing: its capacity to act as a signal about market activity (i.e., levels of supply and demand), and to alert people to the most competitive prices, is substantially diluted when a given price may also incorporate data about a consumer's residential address (and therefore their likely wealth or class background), type of phone or computer operating system, typical amounts spent in a given transaction, and so on.

This 'datafication' of price also represents a significant break with some of the traditional *social* aspects of market organization. Since around the middle of the nineteenth century, fixed prices for goods and open ticketing (making price information clear and public) have been central features of many consumer societies, replacing the interpersonal negotiation and haggling that preceded them. While some types of pricing – notably in insurance – have included 'personalized' elements for much longer, and other types of exchange (notably the second-hand car market) have retained some elements of negotiation and haggling, in general the dominance of fixed, open prices contributed to a gradual 'depersonalization' of economic life (Carrier 1994) and the sense of a roughly 'egalitarian' and open marketplace, in which 'my money's as good as anyone else's', and, crucially, 'all members of … society had access to certain kinds of knowledge' (Turow 2006: 2).

Of course, the fixed, open prices that dominated during this period were not only linked to factors of supply and demand. Pricing has often had a strongly communicative component, as many marketers recognize, and this is particularly true for certain product sectors, such as luxury or 'positional' goods, where part of the utility of a good may derive from the price paid for it (the 'Veblen effect'). Prices also reflect costs more closely in some sectors than others, and mark-ups may vary according to a number of factors including levels of concentration and therefore market power (see, e.g., Schechter 2017). What is more, in areas where some element of face-to-face bargaining or haggling persisted (e.g., the car market) there has long been evidence of price discrimination on the basis of race or ethnicity (e.g., Ayres and Siegelman 1995).

Now, however, ubiquitous data collection about consumers, including the combination of transactional data with data from brokers, has allowed new possibilities for price discrimination, that is, the use of information about consumers to charge them different prices for the same goods or services (Davies 2014; see also OFT 2013: 6), or price steering, that is, providing search results that prioritize goods at a certain price level. The data used in these calculations may include transactional data (including loyalty card data), browsing history, device or operating system used (e.g., Mac, PC, type of mobile device), credit history and various types of behavioural data (e.g., driving behaviour or health and fitness data). It allows companies with sufficient computing infrastructure to modulate prices to reflect knowledge about the consumer. From the perspective of the consumer's information and communication environment, what is striking is that the data itself is often collected without people being aware of it, and that it becomes increasingly difficult to know what prices other people have paid for particular goods.

The goal of price personalization is usually the capture of 'consumer surplus', that is, narrowing the gap between what someone actually paid and the maximum that they might have been willing to pay. To do this, companies are increasingly trying to mobilize all of the types of data outlined above to ensure purchase but also ensure that the price for any given purchase is maximized. Hence if users of Apple iPhones are known to be, on average, wealthier than users of other smartphones, this knowledge can be incorporated into the price. If a company also happens to know (or is able to infer) that you live in a relatively wealthy neighbourhood, this provides an even clearer picture. And if you have previously spent large amounts with the same company (or indeed another one, should that information be available), then a company may feel very comfortable indeed in keeping its prices high for you. Conversely, however, some commentators have worried that price 'personalization' will be used quite differently: to privilege the wealthy and drive poorer people out of the market. The logic of this argument is that companies will offer better discounts, and more competitive prices, to the most desirable consumers in order to retain them, and leave less 'valuable' (i.e., poorer) consumers to 'take it or leave it' at a price set by companies (Turow 2011). This would be consistent with the fact that, historically, the wealthiest people have often received the best terms and conditions in trade (McClain and Mears 2012; Spang 2016). Yet most economists claim the point of price discrimination is not to exclude consumers, but to bring more of them *into* the market. In this scenario, everyone would be paying the maximum they are willing to pay, but for some people that maximum would be a lot higher than others.

Technologies for fluctuating prices can be used for other purposes too. At the moment, behavioural data is used mainly in insurance pricing, i.e., the pricing of risk. Some companies in the UK offer younger drivers the opportunity of having a 'black box' in their car which monitors driving style and feeds the data back into insurance premiums, so that these can be calculated more 'precisely' rather than on broad demographic factors (i.e., the fact that young men are on average the most dangerous drivers) (Economist 2015). Similar developments are being trialled in health insurance (McFall 2019; McFall and Moor 2019). There are also, increasingly, forms of price fluctuation that are not 'personal' at all. In UK supermarkets, some claim that paper price labels will soon be replaced by electronic price displays, which allow more rapidly fluctuating prices and the importing of 'surge' pricing techniques from digital platforms to offline spaces (Morley 2017). These developments create efficiencies for supermarkets, since the ability to adjust prices frequently makes it less likely that they will be left with unsellable inventory at the end of the day. But it also makes it easier to extract maximum prices from consumers, since it enables 'surge' pricing for certain products at certain times – umbrellas when it's raining, ice cream on hot days, petrol during the school run, and so on.

In cases like this one, and others in this chapter, the production of economic information increasingly takes place as a by-product of other, ostensibly 'non-economic', activities, often behind the backs of consumers, without their participation, through systems and categories that they do not understand and of whose existence they are unaware. And yet the implications of these technologies for our economic lives are substantial. Of course, no analysis of these developments is complete without also thinking about how ordinary consumers factor such possibilities into their own behaviour and actions (see Couldry et al. 2016). The kinds of sites and spaces that allow consumers to share information, to challenge particular commercial activities or to consider alternatives to them are also part of the same infrastructure, and point us to the tensions and variegations within this environment. But as Fourcade and Healy (2017) note, scholars should be cautious of assuming that the obstacles to full implementation – whether they come from consumers or from the bluntness of the instruments themselves – will solve the problems of stratification that such infrastructures promote. This echoes a point made by Beer (2009: 997), that it is not clear that the cultural studies language of 'resistance' is the most useful way to capture what is happening when reflexive users shape their profiles 'so as to anticipate the effects the information they provide might have and steer things in the direction they wish'. There are of course many tactics of 'obfuscation' (Brunton and Nissenbaum 2015) that users can draw upon, but the point of these is that they become necessary because of an existing situation of stark information asymmetry, and because people are 'unable to refuse or deny observation' (2015: 7) by more powerful others.

Conclusion

This chapter has focused on a type of communicative act – informing – that is central to the functioning of a market system, and also, in principle, one of the most open and non-directive. And yet, as we have seen, information constructs economic life in quite ambivalent and contradictory ways. There are clearly new *volumes* of information: some of these simply remedy the gaps left as face-to-face commercial communication declines, but others genuinely enhance the possibility for 'voice' among consumers. And in some cases, the new volumes of information create the possibility of new economic communities and publics, capable of autonomous development and self-expression. And yet these new volumes of information risk becoming what Andrejevic (2013) calls 'infoglut', raising questions about how we should assess the credibility or meaningfulness of information when there is so much of it to find and when we don't always know much about its source. Similarly, new information systems have produced new types of exchange. 'Platform' economies depend on the information-gathering capacities of digital networks, and offer many advantages to both buyers and sellers, although they may also create forms of 'lock-in' and become anti-competitive over time. And innovations in digital currencies may well ultimately help consumers by facilitating the growth of distributed digital systems for storing information about transactions and agreements, in ways that protect their privacy. Even here, however, there is some concern that the same technology that currently distributes knowledge and protects privacy may over time be used to track and control what and how people spend.

These cases dramatize a theme that has run throughout this chapter, about the tension between state and corporate power, on the one hand, and the autonomy and freedom of ordinary people with regard to their economic lives on the other. This can be seen in questions about who is best able to control and make use of the new volumes of data and information, and new opportunities for communication, that flow from digital technologies, and of how communication itself is changing in an era when so much of economic action is mediated via digital systems. This is vividly illustrated by the cases of marketing discrimination, and particularly price discrimination and personalization, explored later in the chapter. Here the privatization and capture of data flows, and the entirely proprietary systems of information ownership that flow from them, ultimately create significant and potentially damaging information asymmetries. These have consequences for how customers are treated (e.g., the level of service they receive, or how long it takes to answer their calls or emails), but also for their material wellbeing, since data collected about them behind their back may be used in arriving at credit scores and in formulating 'personalized' prices that are intended to maximize the likelihood of purchase as well as the profit derived from it. As I have suggested above, the possibility that price *itself* may no longer serve as a reliable form of market information is part of a broader shift in which the market sphere loses some of its quasi-public, open quality and becomes more explicitly a battleground, riven by envy and suspicion (Turow 2006).

At the heart of this chapter is the fact that much of the economic 'communication' that now goes on is between machines (or between machines and people) rather than people, and that it takes the form of data or information being collected and used behind our backs. Just as the possibility that people are talking about us behind our backs tends to make us anxious in the rest of our lives, the suspicion that this is happening online (where such 'talk' can be preserved for ever, and even bought and sold) is deeply threatening. The question of how unknown others see you, what they know about you, and how they are going to use that information is a profound one that deserves serious attention. Even in an era of apparent information abundance, there are still significant problems linked to information asymmetry; indeed, there is reason to believe that in some respects this problem is getting worse. As Andrejevic (2013: 5) notes, such a landscape, 'in which only the few have access to the infrastructure for storing and making sense of large amounts of data' is one that has significant societal implications. This is especially true in our economic lives, where digital tools clearly have the potential to deepen the reach of the market.

Taken together, the issues outlined in this chapter suggest that 'informing' may not be so benign a category of communication as it first appears. In its everyday usage it has the ring of democracy, freedom and non-coercion, and yet the practical manipulations of data and information that we have observed in this chapter suggest another sense of the term 'informing', to do with the telling of secrets to more powerful authorities, in ways that may allow those authorities to harm you. It would therefore be simplistic to suggest that new ways of mediating economic life simply 'extend information' in the sense of making more things available; they also have the potential to fundamentally change the power balance in particular relationships, and to institute new social forms and categories. And yet, as with the cases of promotion and persuasion described in the previous chapter, 'informing' does not sit alone in our economic lives, and must exist alongside other forms of communication and speech. To illustrate some of the alternatives to information, I turn in the next chapter to the quite different case of narrative.

Chapter 5

Narrative

Narrative, as a mode of discourse, promises to stitch our economic lives together – making connections, giving context and assigning meaning. Narratives provide the semiotic substance that allows us to make sense of what might otherwise seem a disconnected set of transactions or calculations. And while narrative seems to have little in common with the subject of the last chapter, it shares with information the quality of being relatively open and non-coercive in relation to an audience. Both have a logic of dissemination rather than dialogue (Peters 1999). On the other hand, narrating does not share information's connotation of neutrality; to narrate something is to frame it in a particular way. Narrative involves the representation of an event or series of events and, more specifically, 'the *dramatic imitating and plotting* of human action' (Kearney 2002: 3, emphasis added). Narratives, in other words, are inevitably mediated. They entail choosing what to say, how to say it, what to leave out, and so on. In this respect, narrative shares something with the sociological concept of the 'frame'. What narrative emphasizes, however, is the inter-subjective nature of these framings. Narratives are quintessentially communicative: they are 'someone telling something to someone about something' (Kearney 2002: 5).

   In this chapter I can focus on only two types of economic narrative, and in choosing them I have deliberately avoided the narratives about the macro economy that typically receive the most attention in communication studies. Instead, I focus, first, on fictional narratives about economic themes found in literature, film and television, and then secondly on the kinds of narratives – typically a blend of fiction and non-fiction – that economic actors produce in order to explain or justify their actions and to help them make decisions. Fictional narratives often reflect the particular concerns of their place and time, but they may also embody longstanding moral precepts about money's corrosive, or potentially corrosive, nature. There are some important variations according to genre and medium – as we shall see, feature films may be limited in how they portray the subtleties of economic life in ways that novels, for example, are not. Nonetheless, in fictional narratives we often find a form of mass communication that is either hostile to capitalism, or that routinely questions its effects on workers, consumers, families and relationships. As such, fiction is frequently a force for value plurality in economic life, even though it is rarely studied explicitly as a form of economic communication.[1]

Next, I examine the narratives produced by economic actors – ranging from amateur investors to art dealers and large companies – to explain their actions, to affirm their identities and to help them make decisions, as well as to give their economic behaviour a sense of meaning and purpose. These narratives may be produced in the context of face-to-face transactions, in official reports and promotions, or during deliberations and decision-making processes. But in almost all of these contexts, the narration of economic life involves an attempt to add context or meaning to an action or calculation, and to root economic behaviour in a wider system of values. In these contexts, narratives are usually a force for the *embeddedness* of economic action in social life (Polanyi 2001 [1944]) rather than its abstraction. Such efforts may be more or less credible, and, as we shall see, many economic narratives are simply instances of what Habermas (1984) calls strategic action. Nonetheless, they all reflect a shared understanding that economic activity and the calculations that accompany it cannot become too far removed from more substantive social meanings before they become alienating.

Between these two sections, the chapter explores how economic narratives came to be defined as either fictional or non-fictional in the first place. Here I draw on Mary Poovey's (2008) account of the history of economic writing, and her claim that an early 'fact/fiction continuum' was gradually replaced by a clearer distinction between genres. For Poovey, what is at stake in all economic inscription is the claim to be able to mediate *value*, and over time forms of economic writing became functionally specialized, so that they either claim to mediate value in different ways, or model different value systems altogether. This historical account is particularly useful in understanding why some economists (as well as economic sociologists and others) have recently displayed a 'turn to narrative' to understand different aspects of economic life. The chapter concludes with a brief discussion of claims that narrative is in decline or in peril. Here I explore arguments that narrative is in tension with information, as a way of knowing the world, and consider how far economic narratives might be challenged by the rise of data-based ways of knowing described in the preceding chapter.

Narratives, stories and why they matter

Narratives and stories are fundamental to human life. Their most important function is to 'shape time according to human priorities' (Abbott 2008: 4; see also Bruner 2004 [1987]). In contrast to 'clock time', narrative deals in 'events and incidents' (Abbott 2008: 13) and this capacity to represent an event according to one's own understanding of its significance is what defines it. The 'art of storytelling', for Aristotle, involves 'the dramatic imitating and plotting of human action' and through this process 'haphazard happenings' are made memorable over time (Kearney 2002: 3). Narrative is often distinguished from simple 'history', however, since historical writing has little freedom to invent without evidence, and is constrained by the existence of sources that it should not contradict without good reason (Fludernik 2009: 3). Yet historical writing shares with narrative the sense of having a perspective – it comes from a particular person, place and time – and thus as being a *mediation*, something that 'comes between us and the world' (Abbott 2008: 154), directing our attention to some parts and not others.

Narratives and stories also have an ideological function. For Lévi-Strauss, they were ways of providing 'symbolic solutions to contradictions which could not be solved empirically' (Kearney 2002: 6). This, as we shall see, is a useful perspective on the way that economic questions are represented in fiction, and is a key assumption of ideology critique. In this view, happy endings in stories about poverty, or 'just desserts' for greedy characters in films, defuse in the symbolic world something that may be less easily resolved in the real world. The more optimistic account of narrative is that it also has the ability to change our minds and to shift us away from comfortable or comforting beliefs. The 'creative redescription of the world' that defines narrative's mimetic function may be a way of domesticating the world and making the complex comprehensible, or the unbearable palatable, but at its best it also allows 'hidden patterns and hitherto unexplored meanings' to unfold (Kearney 2002: 12–13). It may enable us to empathize with characters who suffer, while giving sufficient aesthetic distance to allow us to discern the 'hidden causes of things' and the greater philosophical truths underpinning the action.

Arguments about narrative's role in sense making may apply to the individual as well as to the community. Narrative is believed to provide us with 'one of our most viable forms of *identity*' (Kearney 2002: 4) because it offers a 'pattern to cope with the experience of chaos and confusion' (p. 129), as well as a structure – beginning, middle, end – that seems to mirror human life itself. And as Carolyn Steedman (1986: 6) notes, the stories we tell about ourselves – about how we have come to be the person we are, or in the place that we are – are often a form of political analysis in miniature, a way of connecting individual history to national or world history. They may also be in conflict with the 'official interpretive devices of a culture'. When we tell our own story, we may find ourselves offering explanations for events, or justifications for actions and decisions, that run counter to standard ways of understanding things.

Narratives are also constrained by their form and genre and by the contexts and audiences for their telling. This places certain limits on *how* they can reveal the world. As Stuart Hall points out, even the most graphic and terrible events, if recounted within the genre of a children's story, will almost inevitably have a 'happy ending';[2] in that sense, meanings are 'already concealed or held within the forms of the stories themselves' (1984: 7). Just as the factual narratives of television news are constrained in how they report economic issues by a series of conventions, time constraints, assumptions about the audience, and so on, so the genre conventions of drama, epic, saga, comedy and farce also exert their own pressures. Form as well as content matters in determining what narratives – including economic narratives – can do.

Literary fiction and the repudiation of the market

Fictional narratives about the economy have often adopted a sceptical attitude to the personal and social effects of capitalism and commerce. To understand why this is so, it is useful to consider the historical relationship between creative writers and moral views of market society (Fourcade and Healy 2007). Before the nineteenth century, it was those on the right of the political spectrum who most commonly opposed commerce and the desire for enrichment; support for 'prestige' values was under these circumstances support for the nobility or landowning classes against the alternative figures of the merchant or 'cosmopolitan' (Delany 2002; see also Hirschman 1970). Of course, writers had their own interests in money – 'both as a force in society and as the reward for their enterprises' (Delany 2002: 13) – but their status position was such that they more often cherished the 'prestige order' than whatever might follow it, and were sympathetic to those, such as Matthew Arnold, who saw commerce as hostile to 'culture'. At the same time, the question of how intensified commercial activity might affect the structures of social life was a real and vibrant one for authors writing from the eighteenth century onwards.

This can be traced not just in the works of successive writers, but in the evolution of particular writers' ideas over time.

One example of this is the popularity of the 'marriage plot' novel in nineteenth-century England, which, as Elsie Michie notes, was a kind of mythic structure, or abstract pattern, through which a broader 'fear of accumulation' could be explored and potentially worked through 'at the level of structure, action, and characterization' (2011: 6). This fear of accumulation was, more specifically, a fear of what wealth might do to the human personality and the structure of human relationships; it was also a set of questions about what kinds of personal traits or social values might be necessary to counteract or moderate the power of commerce. Indeed, Mary Poovey (2008: 85) suggests that the 'evaluation of character' – something that novels taught, but that 'everyone who accepted a token of credit was required to do' – was at the heart of imaginative writing's claim to mediate the credit economy. It is for this reason that the marriage plot focuses on the area of romantic relationships: it foregrounds the anxiety about 'economic developments in the place where we least expect or want to find those materialist concerns' (Michie 2011: xiii).

As Michie shows, through a focus on Jane Austen, the marriage plot dramatizes these anxieties by setting up a plot in which a male (or, less commonly, female) hero, in order to be virtuous, must choose a spouse in a way that does not make the 'vulgar question of money' the prime concern. Michie suggests that the figure of female heiress, or rich woman, is an especially important figure in Austen's works, since she personifies the alternative that a person of great wealth might present to the 'genteelly impoverished' female character that the plot has set up as more appropriate. This figure changes over time, as Austen herself appears to take the attractions of wealth more seriously. In *Pride and Prejudice* (1813), for example, Miss Bingley and Lady Catherine de Bourgh are 'drawn in larger than life, almost caricatured terms', and in *Sense and Sensibility* (1811), Mrs John Dashwood is a rather grotesque figure, revealed as 'narrow-minded, selfish and greedy' (pp. 24–8). By the time of *Mansfield Park* (1814), however, while there are still some 'crassly comic figures' of rich women, Mary Crawford is full of 'energy and élan' (p. 31) – something Austen's readers are invited to appreciate – and is 'so appealing that the novel's hero almost marries her' (p. 24).

Interestingly, by the time of *Emma* (1815), the rich woman has in fact become the protagonist, and Michie shows that it is Emma's own attitudes and behaviours vis-à-vis others that must undergo a change in order for the plot's relational dilemmas to be resolved. Over the course of the novel,

Emma moves from 'happy self-involvement' to coming to perceive the injuries that she has done to women poorer than herself. By making the rich woman, Emma, the central character, the 'self-interest triggered by wealth' can be 'embedded at a deeper and more psychological level than is true of the rich women in ... previous novels' (pp. 31–2). Nonetheless, whereas the personality dimensions of wealth remain fairly stable in *Sense and Sensibility*, Emma's psychology is able to change as she works through who and what she is in relation to less fortunate others. It is because she has been 'taught to make the mental gesture of acknowledging the equality of others' (p. 59) that a happy ending for Emma is possible.

'Marriage plot'-style stories remain immensely popular. Michie's explanation for this is that while the marriage plot may originally have been a 'literary structure that parallels the rise and fall of British economic dominance' (in the latter parts of her study she examines the work of Henry James, where heiresses are both more likeable and predominantly American), over time it loses its association with a particular time and place, and comes instead to function as a looser configuration: an 'identifiable sequence ... comprising a virtually infinite complex of works' (Badiou, cited on p. 216). At this point it becomes 'a structure that feels natural or self-evident rather than one that seems pointedly to comment on contemporary events' (p. 216). In other words, while marriage plots have an identifiable history in commenting on the tension between aristocratic and commercial values, and trying to find a 'moral' way through them, they circulate now as though they are timeless, becoming part of the repertoire of narrative devices that can be deployed in a variety of contexts and combinations.

One reason for the continued popularity of this narrative device may simply be that the determinants of happy relationships are a persistent concern for people regardless of time and place, and that, especially in strongly class- or caste-based societies, people will endlessly return to stories that dramatize the possibilities of love outwitting social structures and monetary power. Michie herself alludes to Freud's notion of 'working through' when she describes how novelists' attitudes to the figure of the rich woman gradually change over time. Yet it is worth remembering that in Freud's account, 'working through' is counter-posed to processes of remembering and repeating (Freud 1958 [1914]): from this perspective, repetition of the same story over and over again – as in the endless re-telling of the 'marriage plot' – is precisely what happens when one is *unable* to work through something (or, in Freud's view, to properly remember and acknowledge what is traumatic about it). The point for Freud is that if one had genuinely 'worked through' a particular question or anxiety, there would be no need to keep re-enacting or repeating it.

Seen in this light, the endless repetition of stories and narratives in which protagonists transcend the power of money, social structure and class division through their own virtuous personal qualities looks less like 'working through' and more like what Lévi-Strauss described as offering 'symbolic solutions to problems that could not be solved empirically' (Kearney 2002: 6). In a world in which money and class origin largely determine life chances, and 'assortative mating' is a social fact (e.g., Henz and Mills 2018), to insistently tell stories in which love conquers all and neither money nor class are a barrier to personal happiness seems more like a comforting fantasy than a meaningful working through of reality. Of course, the subtle differences between versions of the marriage plot matter: it matters if rich people can be portrayed as sympathetic, if the personal qualities necessary to overcome the potential corruptions of wealth change over time, or if stories come to see a 'happy ending' as one in which people marry within their own class (as in *Emma*). Furthermore, details along the way may matter as much as the overall 'resolution'; elements or scenes that are part of a narrative may in some cases be more revealing or resonant than its overall structure. The point, however, is that the endless re-telling of some version of more or less the same story suggests that the 'working through' of that story is very much ongoing, rather than complete.

To explore this idea further, consider a more ambivalent story about money, relationships and personal virtue, set in 1980s London. Alan Hollinghurst's *The Line of Beauty* was published in 2004 but deals with the period leading up to the 'Big Bang' and concerns the fate of Nick Guest, an 'aspirant middle-class Oxford graduate' who spends the summer of 1983 in the wealthy west London home of a university friend and then stays for four years. In Nicky Marsh's (2007) study, she shows that although Nick's professed interests are aesthetic rather than financial (he is doing a PhD in literature at UCL, while many of his contemporaries work in business or finance), he is deeply impressed by his wealthy friend's family, and longs to fit in. However, both his class position and sexuality make this awkward. When he begins a relationship with Wani, the son of a wealthy Lebanese businessman, his own relationship to money gradually begins to shift: he takes 'a surprising pleasure' in Wani's ostentatious luxury flat, and 'the sexual and financial pleasures of this relationship are shown to be deeply interdependent and deeply compromising of Nick's disinterested aesthetic sensibilities' (Marsh 2007: 88).

While Nick participates in the many advantages of wealth via his relationship with Wani, and his innocence about money is shown to be little more than a function of his privilege (Marsh 2007), the approaching threat of HIV combined with the stigma around his sexuality mean that while Nick is undeniably complicit in the world of the Feddens, he is also vulnerable in ways that they are not. As Marsh (2007) notes, if the narrative arc of Hollinghurst's novel allows the risks of HIV and the risks of high finance to be read together, 'it is only in order that he can make apparent the significant differences between the ways in which they have both constructed communities and notions of risk'. When it is revealed that Gerald Fedden has had an affair and is accused of financial malpractice, 'the viral capacities of the money economy and AIDS are demonstrated to have violently antithetical consequences' (p. 91): money protects the Feddens, but Nick is thrown out of the house and faces the death of his partner and his own imminent mortality, something from which his own growing wealth and inheritance from Wani cannot protect him.

Compared to 'marriage plots', narratives such as Hollinghurst's are altogether more ambivalent, and perhaps for that reason do not lend themselves to endless re-workings: they are unlikely to become part of the inventory of narrative tropes described by Hall. As Marsh points out, Hollinghurst dismantles the too-easy opposition between money and culture that is so often used to criticize capitalism or the wealthy (and that was a motivating tension for fiction in the eighteenth and nineteenth centuries). He also subverts the simplistic parallels that are often made between money and sex (e.g., that they are both a 'currency', a 'language' or a form of power) and shows that the consequences of perceived sexual impropriety are very different for the wealthy Gerald Fedden and middle-class Nick, and that money's protective powers are far more substantial (although not limitless). Hollinghurst's narrative offers a more complete 'working through' of its subject matter; it has not 'conveniently forgotten' certain facts about the 1980s, but instead has revealed them in their ugly complexity and sadness.

Filmic and televisual narratives about money

While novels are in some ways suited to this kind of subtlety, visual media – and in particular film – face various obstacles in representing economic life. Many aspects of capitalist activity are hard to see: they are 'immaterial and systemic', and while they depend on connectivity, these connections occur behind the scenes (Kinkle and Toscano 2011). Similarly, the consequences of economic crises are hard to visualize on screen; an article in *Life* magazine in 1936 lamented the difficulty of capturing the Depression photographically, since it consisted of 'things not happening, business not being done' (cited on p. 40). Showing the causal elements behind financial crashes is also difficult, not because they are not known, but because the financial instruments responsible for the 2008 crash (to take one example) were both mathematically complicated and hard to describe or to see.

Filmmakers have tried to resolve these problems in a range of ways. Finance may be hard to visualize but it does at least lend itself to high drama. Early films such as *L'Argent* (1929) used montage techniques to show the speed of communication and information flows on the trading floor of a stock exchange (Kinkle and Toscano 2011). In more recent films such as *The Big Short* (2016), there are cut-away shots in which a celebrity figure explains complex financial terms through a more accessible analogy, such as Anthony Bourdain explaining collateralized debt obligations (CDOs) through a parallel with making a fish stew out of old and past-their-best pieces of fish. Other Hollywood films have approached aspects of contemporary economic systems more indirectly: *Up In the Air* (2009) dramatized the distance between management and workers by focusing on the literal spatial gaps between a life spent 'up in the air', or in the non-places of airports, and one spent 'on the ground'. *The Florida Project* (2017) likewise uses the physical space of a budget motel on a highway outside Disney World to focus in depth on the everyday lives of low-income families and to dramatize the gap between their material lives and the fantasies offered by mass media and culture.

As Kinkle and Toscano point out, focusing on architecture and space can actually convey the alienations of capitalism very effectively, but it is far more common for filmmakers to rely on plot – and specifically, the use of 'morality tales' – to make arguments about the workings of market society. In this context, one strategy is to contrast 'the virtues of the firm, based on real skills and assets, against the depredations of profit and finance' (2011: 42). This, they imply, is fine so far as it goes, but the problem is that it tends to romanticize 'proper' capitalism and then criticizes finance for 'perverting' it. Hollywood films in particular prefer not to imagine any *inherent* conflicts between capital and labour, and instead offer moral narratives that contrast 'proper' work with deviant finance. Perhaps most commonly of all, the moral force of films about money and business often comes from the family: the corrupting potential of money and finance is compared with, and can often only be mitigated by, the values of home and family ties. Kinkle and Toscano suggest that this ignores the 'collusion between the ideology of the family, home ownership, and commodity consumption' (p. 45), but a more fundamental problem is that in portraying 'kith and kin' as benign and nurturing, these binaries may also misrepresent and mystify the nature of family life.

It is also worth considering how forms other than film may be able to do different kinds of things in their narrative treatment of money. Televisual narratives, for example, may still employ various kinds of morality tale when representing money and the economy, but they can do so over a longer duration and in ways that show greater conflict and complexity along the way. Similarly, longer-running drama series and serials may be able to show the fallout from economic crises, for example, in ways that a ninety-minute or two-hour film may not. Since televisual narratives require less obvious, and less concentrated, 'high drama' than the average Hollywood film, they also have less need to turn to themes of big business and finance, and can be more concerned with 'lay' or everyday economic activities. Popular soap operas – such as *Coronation Street* or *EastEnders* in the UK – with their focus on the mundane lives of ordinary people, are far more likely to show economic activity as a routine and embedded (in the Polanyian sense) part of everyday life – something that takes place in pubs, corner shops and market stalls – than most films, and even many novels, ever are. And their slow, gradual unfolding quality means that the fallout from unemployment or debt can be revealed in something approaching the incremental way it typically unfolds in everyday life.

There are also a number of more critically acclaimed series in which we can see the 'everydayness' of certain economic arrangements, and a focus on the way that individual lives are shaped by wider social and economic forces. In *The Wire* (2002–8), for example, each series deals with a different institution in the city of Baltimore – the drugs trade, the docks, city hall, the education system, journalism – but those institutions are approached as a set of social and economic relations, with hierarchies, ways of working and a distinct economic logic. Interestingly, one of the writers of the show, David Simon, described *The Wire* as a 'visual novel' (cited in Penfold-Mounce et al. 2011: 154). Each 'chapter', it is implied, can explore themes more fully – and perhaps in a more literary way – than would be possible in a film. This allows the presentation of social and economic relations in a way that is 'closer to that of complexity theory ... with its strong emphasis on the unpredictability of patterns of emergence and the difficulties of understanding causality' (pp. 163–4).

The fact/fiction continuum in economic writing

At this point I want to turn to a different set of arguments about narrative, concerning its role in constituting or supporting (rather than reflecting or reporting on) economic activity. In recent years a number of works have addressed the linguistic and rhetorical strategies used in economic writing in general, and economic theory in particular (e.g., McCloskey 1983; Mirowski 1989; Klamer and Leonard 1994; see also chapter 3), as well as the representations of economic concepts in literature (Woodmansee and Osteen 1999; Marsh 2007). There has also been growing interest in using the concept of narrative to explain how people frame and make sense of economic events. Such interest can be traced in texts by leading economists (e.g., Shiller 2005; Bénabou et al. 2018) but also in studies of business and in the work of economic sociologists. The interest in narrative is, for reasons I will come on to, especially pronounced in relation to finance, but it is increasingly used to think about other kinds of economic activity too.

To understand how narratives are used in these contexts, but also why that might have been a strange thing to do until fairly recently, it is useful to consider how different kinds of economic writing have developed historically. Mary Poovey has explained this development as a process of *generic differentiation*: that is, 'the gradual elaboration of sets of conventions and claims about method that were intended to differentiate between kinds of writing' (2008: 1). At the heart of this process was the emergence of the distinction between fact and fiction, replacing a more complex 'fact/fiction continuum' that preceded it. As Poovey shows, even as late as the last quarter of the eighteenth century, many forms of writing 'did not systematically distinguish between what we call fact and fiction' (2008: 28–9); these included news ballads and 'broadsides', meditations, allegories, natural histories, 'Providence books', spiritual biographies and more. At the same time, the introduction of new sorts of monetary instruments and tokens – which derived their value from 'fictions' of various kinds – had to be carefully managed and their stylistic features organized so that users could distinguish between 'good' (valid) and 'bad' (invalid) tokens.

The development of different genres of economic narrative can thus be understood as a process of 'fictionalization' and 'factualization' by which writers sought to distinguish types of writing, thereby creating hierarchies both within and between them. There were many drivers of these processes, but the rise of financial writing as a genre, for example, could be traced not just to the growing number of people for whom financial information and commentary would be useful, but also, in the wake of the South Sea Bubble of 1720, a 'backlash against financial instruments that seemed to harbor, much less turn on, fictions of any kind' (2008: 82). It is in this context that new genres of financial writing, including financial news, 'business opinion', financial journalism and, later, investment advice, came to prominence. The development of factual genres of economic writing – designed to 'authenticate ... informational and/or theoretical knowledge' – was, then, at least in part a response to the 'fictional' nature of certain new kinds of economic activity and the 'lies and secrets' that seemed to typify the economic activities of traders and 'stockjobbers' (pp. 80–3).

At the other end of the fact/fiction continuum, imaginative writers at this time also began to renounce the blurring of fact and fiction and to develop characters with no real-life referents, as part of an effort to distinguish and elevate literary writing, and to advance a specifically aesthetic model of value. This, as Poovey shows, entailed the development of particular stylistic features – for example, 'call[ing] attention to their own artistry' (p. 29), or using 'novelistic language' that would invoke poetry rather than informational writing – and ways of managing the narrative that sought to ensure that readers would not stray beyond the text in making sense of it (pp. 358–62). To the extent that these genres were still involved in 'mediating' the credit economy of their time, they did so through the building of suspense and ambiguity, and by encouraging readers to engage in the 'evaluation of character' (p. 85).

These developments led to a gradual but definitive shift in the relation of different kinds of writing to *value*: at the start of the period Poovey considers, all genres of economic writing – imaginative, financial, monetary – were concerned with helping people to understand the new credit economy and the market model of value it promoted. At this point, there was much traffic between fact and fiction, with fictional writers drawing on financial 'plot lines' and other economic writers borrowing 'tropes and narrative conventions from imaginative writers when they encountered economic phenomena that defied the discipline's ordinary explanatory paradigms' (Poovey 2008: 9; see also Knight 2013: 6). Over time, their ways of 'mediating' value became more functionally specialized: monetary genres such as coins, credit papers and paper notes were seem to 'embody' value; financial writing came to represent, explain or comment on that value; while literary writing – although sometimes taking the market as its theme, and certainly embroiled in it through the publishing industry – developed a moral or aesthetic model of value that seemed to repudiate market value and position itself as an alternative. The relative prestige of fact-based genres in mediating value explains the higher disciplinary status of economics as compared to literary studies, so Poovey claims, but it also enables literature's ongoing claim to uniqueness as a form of disinterested critique (2008: 3).

It is in this context that the contemporary interest in the narrative features of economic life – from economists to marketers to economic sociologists and anthropologists – is to be understood. Narratives may have been used in the works of early political economists but after the marginal revolution, and with economics modelling itself on physics and mathematics, the explanatory role of narrative receded. Nor would people's *own* narratives about the economy have been as of much interest to economists as they are to sociologists. Until fairly recently economics has concerned itself primarily with manifest behaviours, rather than with underlying psychological processes or beliefs. However, as behavioural economics has shown systematic deviations from the presumed rationality of economic theory, some economists have become more interested in the ways that rational action is either enabled or inhibited. As part of this move, they have also become interested in the role of narratives in the formation of economic beliefs.

The economy as a narrated phenomenon

This interest in narrative is particularly noticeable in the area of financial markets. This is perhaps unsurprising given that – as Poovey suggests – it has long borne a complex relation to the fact/fiction divide. As I noted in chapter 2, Robert Shiller has built on Keynes's notion of 'animal spirits' to speculate about the role of stories and narratives in inflating the dot-com bubble of the late 1990s, and argued that the news media play a particular important role in the circulation of narratives 'by attaching new stories to stock market movements ... thereby enhancing the salience of these movements' (2005: 95). In his work with Akerlof (2009), he treats narratives as an innate quality of the human mind, and the basis of memory and knowledge. Indeed, most economic accounts of narrative tend to make them psychological, rather than cultural or literary, phenomena (see also Bénabou et al. 2018). This makes them easier to model, but it cannot easily account for the variations – e.g., by genre, medium or context – that other disciplines take more seriously and that, arguably, make narratives interesting in the first place.

Economic sociologists have also been interested in the role of narratives in shaping financial behaviour, but have offered more empirical detail than the broad-brush picture painted by Shiller. Harrington (2008), for example, suggests that while many accounts of stock market dynamics – including Shiller's – foreground the human capacity for imitative behaviour, one can often discern more subtle social and identity dynamics behind this. In her study of amateur investor clubs, she suggests that members do not straightforwardly 'imitate' each other, but rather have to negotiate their way through a 'marketplace of stories' in deciding where to invest. This involves weighing up the (often competing) views of analysts about a stock's value and profit potential with the views of publicly traded firms, but it also involves discussion and deliberation within the investment club itself, often supplemented by the 'narrative templates' provided by the national association (Harrington 2008: 51–2). Clea Bourne (2017) notes that stock market investing in fact requires a certain amount of 'story-telling' to keep it going, since its products are essentially invisible and also quite hard to represent. Twenty-four-hour financial television channels such as Bloomberg may be particularly useful media for such storytelling, because they can produce a constant supply of fast-moving stories and visualize them in interesting ways. Alternatively, financial PR specialists may be employed to shape the 'story' of a particular product or firm in ways that are consistent with its brand positioning as either trustworthy and dependable or adventurous and daring.

It is not only in the sphere of finance that narratives constitute economic action as meaningful. Another example comes from the art world. Olav Velthuis has shown how prices here are made meaningful through the narratives of art dealers in particular. In art worlds, he shows, prices rarely provide their signalling or informational function in isolation, but are embedded within stories, which give them meaning and provide an 'ornate vocabulary to interpret and characterize' transactions (2005: 136). He identifies three key narratives to have dominated the art market since the 1950s, which get mobilized when dealers are asked to explain prices: a 'tragic' narrative, in which an honourable art world falls prey to capitalism, is used to make sense of sales in which art works started to fetch record prices; a 'superstar' narrative is used to account for and explain high and rapidly increasing prices, particularly in the 1980s; and a narrative of 'prudence' or 'reality' is used to explain dealers' own attempts to shape prices so as to support the long-term careers of their own artists. As Velthuis shows, these stories are not simply 'about' the art market or prices. They also testify to the capabilities of collectors (in selecting pieces whose value increases), describe the development of an artist over time, or express the status of a particular gallery. Narratives about prices, in other words, are not only produced in order to justify them – although that is an important function – but also to allow dealers to communicate something about who they are and to express their relationships with artists and the market as a whole.

Narratives are also part of other elements of business activity, such as marketing. In the case of 'corporate storytelling' (e.g., Fog et al. 2005; Cawthorne 2016; Thier 2018), companies aim to create an affecting story, or set of stories, about their organization or brand, in order to imbue it with depth and meaning, with the hope that consumers and other stakeholders will believe it to possess substantive values and a purpose beyond profit-making. There are variations in how such activities are justified, but most share the assumption that human beings seek meaningfulness, and that companies or brands could be credible sources of meaning in people's lives. As one text puts it:

> When companies and brands communicate through stories they help us to find our way in today's world. They address our emotions and give us the means to express our values … the brand story gradually becomes synonymous with how we define ourselves as individuals, and products become the symbols that we use to tell the story of ourselves. (Fog et al. 2005: 20)

The point, in other words, is to harness the purported human inclination to seek meaning through narrative, and use it to build brand loyalty. In making such claims for narrative, these texts typically rely on well-worn marketing clichés (e.g., the best stories are 'contagious'; the point of marketing is to 'connect emotionally' with consumers), but they also rely on clichés about narrative: for example, that our brains are 'hardwired to tell stories' (Cawthorne 2016: 5), that there are three (or four or five) 'core elements' to every story, that there are a limited number of plotlines, and so on. Tellingly, questions of truthfulness or accuracy – that is, whether the narrative claims to be factual or fictional in nature – are mostly avoided. Instead, such texts offer advice on how to find stories that *work* for a given organization or brand. The search process might include finding stories about the CEO, interviewing employees, finding stories from customers or information about how a product came into existence. In most cases, however, such kernels of truth are merely a starting point for the creation of an elaborate narrative that allows the brand to create an idealized version of itself.

These examples of nonfiction narratives about economic life draw attention to two features of narrative that I have tried to foreground in the chapter so far: one is that narratives – even nonfiction ones – are always fabricated: they are not synonymous with 'events themselves', but rather are a way of mediating them. This is not to claim that nonfiction narratives are necessarily untruthful – they may be constrained, to a greater or lesser degree, by the requirement to have at least some referent to reality (Fludernik 2009) – but they can nonetheless exist on various points along the 'fact/fiction continuum' described by Poovey. This is perhaps most vividly illustrated by the case of 'corporate storytelling', where truthfulness or accuracy is secondary to the more fundamental goal of finding a vehicle for brand values that themselves have an uncertain relationship to 'facts', and will typically have been formulated with the help of a marketing agency. The second point is that these narratives are almost always intended, consciously or not, to add meaning and context to economic activities or calculations that may otherwise seem purely instrumental or abstract. They are in this sense forces for embedding, or embeddedness, and a tacit admission that it is through such embeddedness that we make sense of economic life.

The challenge to narrative

In many ways, narratives are more important than ever. At a time when news circulates rapidly and in fragments, and in which many aspects of our economic lives no longer involve us seeing or talking to other people in order to make financial decisions, it is perhaps unsurprising that narratives seem necessary in order to stitch these fragments together. And yet many see narrative as under threat. Some have challenged the persistence of narrative on normative grounds: narratives, it is said, offer visions of the world that are too neat, too linear or too totalizing (e.g., Abbott 2008). Then there is what might be called the technological challenge to narrative – the fact that many stories no longer have a recognizable linear narrative form. Accounts of ourselves on social media, using photographs, emoji, abbreviations, short video clips – all of which can be heavily edited, filtered, revised or replaced – seem to be drowning 'real' narratives in a multitude of new, non-narrative forms of telling, which threaten to in some way overwhelm or displace it. And yet these kinds of claims have been made for some time. Walter Benjamin wrote about the threat posed to narrativity by the information age; what he seemed to have in mind was not the demise of storytelling as such, but rather the demise of particular forms (Kearney 2002). And there is plenty of evidence to suggest that narratives are still important and popular, even while their forms are subject to change: the popularity of drama series at the same time as the rise of all of these more fragmented technological ways of telling is perhaps revealing about the need for more enduring forms of meaning-making (see also Hayles 2012: 181).

The more serious challenge to narrative in fact comes from the prolif-eration of accounts of the self that are entirely numerical or datafied in nature. These 'data doubles' (whose contours were outlined in the previous chapter) are often more powerful than our real selves when it comes to certain kinds of economic activities, such as getting credit or getting access to particular goods and services. Thus, to the extent that decisions about our economic lives are made on the basis of the application of fixed rules to our personal data (i.e., on the use of algorithms), our *own* accounts of our lives (i.e., our own narratives) may be losing their power and relevance. In this case, what we are seeing is not so much a decline in narrative *per se*, but rather the decreasing importance of the stories we tell about ourselves at a time when data and metrics of various kinds are being used to provide 'objective' information about the self across a range of contexts, from job interviews to loan applications.

This, then, is the paradox of contemporary narrative: that narrative accounts of our lives, whether we produce them or consume those produced by others, seem to be as popular as ever – and even finding new outlets – at a time when they are ostensibly facing their greatest threat from new ways of representing the person and the world. It is tempting, as I have suggested, to see these developments as related: that the rise of abstract and datafied ways of knowing the person is likely to lead to a counter-movement that emphasizes qualitative and contextualized accounts of selfhood. This is the position taken by Katherine Hayles. She is sceptical of claims that the rise of the database and other computational forms will displace narrative, if only because database 'needs narrative to make its results meaningful' (2012: 176). In this respect, the growth of data and datafied ways of knowing is likely to make narratives proliferate 'as they transform to accommodate new data and mutate to probe what lies beyond the exponentially expanding infosphere' (2012: 183). On the other hand, Hayles acknowledges that the place of narrative in our wider culture has changed: where narrative was once a viable explanation for large-scale events, such explanations must now be rooted in data, even if the data is wrapped up in a narrative ('When Ben Bernanke testifies before Congress', says Hayles, referring to a previous Chair of the Federal Reserve, 'he typically does not recount data alone. Rather, he tells a *story*'). And the proliferation of data poses problems for narrative: as databases expand to include new elements, narrative explanations must be constantly revised – something that is not always easy or straightforward. The dominance of data, and the growth of data-centred accounts of the world, may explain the renewed appeal of narrative as sense-making technique, but narrative does not offer a straightforward solution to the problem.

Conclusion

In the context of economic lives often dominated by the remote decisions and abstract calculations of powerful institutions, it is appealing to see fictional or autobiographical narratives as a space of respite: an opportunity for contextual richness, subtlety of thought and attention to local details and feelings. And in some ways this is how Poovey suggests that fictional writers historically saw themselves. It is certainly true that in contrast to the dominance of the persuasive modes of address and datafied ways of knowing described in previous chapters, narrative ways of thinking about our economic lives offer a type of communication and meaning-making that seems to be much needed. Narratives matter because they are where we get our values (Poovey 2008), how we justify our actions and decisions, and how we formulate a sense of identity (Velthuis 2005; Harrington 2008). They are also, very often, concerned with collective sense making, mutual comprehension and memory. And as the various writers discussed in the first part of the chapter have shown, fiction writers historically positioned themselves in opposition to commercial values and the value plurality that fiction offers can be a way of imagining alternative economic futures.

Yet we should not be too romantic or naïve about narrative's possibilities. Imagination and fantasy, as Will Davies notes, are 'internal to the space of calculation', in the sense that the capacity to imagine that which does not yet materially exist is necessary for capitalist expansion and growth (2018b: 22) as well as part of resistance to it. Some of the world's most powerful economic actors have also come to see stories as a way to bridge the gap between their own interests and the interests of those whose lives they seek to govern. 'Corporate storytelling' is now a popular service for business, and is often simply an attempt to dress up the impersonal calculative procedures of large organizations in the guise of something more human or socially embedded. It also shows that our economic lives are still a place where genres blur, and where fact and fiction are to be understood as a continuum rather than as opposing poles. Similarly, as the early parts of this chapter have made clear, there are plenty of critics for whom the fictional narratives of film and literature are likewise spaces of myth making and ideology, offering false comforts and false solutions rather than genuine opportunities to reflect or to gain distance or insight.

For all of this, narrative remains a vital aspect of our economic lives, and a key way in which those lives are communicated and mediated. It is surprising how rarely theories of economic communication take into account the fictional, historical or autobiographical narratives about the economy that surround us, as though the only economic communications that make a difference are the pronouncements of governments or central banks. It is also perhaps telling that the main exception to this, so far, has been in the world of finance, a sphere that in Poovey's (2008) terms has always occupied a complicated position on the fact/fiction continuum. Here, both economists and critics are gradually turning to the concept of narrative to explain how people make sense of an area that often seems mysterious and hard to comprehend (see, e.g., Shiller 2005; Harrington 2008). The argument of this book, however, has been that it is not just in the realms of finance and the macro economy where we need these perspectives. If we want to develop sociological insights into our economic lives – that is, to appreciate how different groups come to understand, talk about or make sense of certain things as 'economic' – then we cannot just look at parts of the economy already seen as important, or at communicative forms already assumed to be powerful. Instead, we must look at more ordinary instances of economic action, and at forms of communication – in fiction, online and in everyday speech – whose contribution to our economic worldview has thus far been underappreciated. This is something I have started to do in this chapter, but that will be explored further in the next, on debate and discussion.

Chapter 6

Discussion

Discussion and debate have long been prized forms of human communication. Thought to be superior to the one-way messages of mass media, they are seen by some as 'the summit of human encounter' (Peters 1999: 33). This elevation of dialogue goes back to the ancient world, but in contemporary times it is most strongly associated with Habermas's work on the public sphere (1989) and communicative rationality (1984, 1987). For Habermas, dialogical interaction is a prototypically democratic form of communication: it emerges from a public sphere of equals and should be clearly distinguished from the promotional or self-advancing forms of communication that were the theme of chapter 3. Participants in a discussion may operate according to different motivations – for example, success-oriented on the one hand, or aimed at reaching mutual understanding on the other – but they typically know the difference: they can distinguish between 'situations in which they are casually exerting influence *upon* others from those in which they are coming to an understanding *with* others' (1984: 286). And the goal of reaching a mutual understanding is seen by many as the foundation of democratic community and justice. This framing of dialogue and discussion continues to be influential in media studies and invites us to view economic discussion in a particular way: as rational, public, political discourse concerning the sources of economic problems and the appropriate goals and methods of economic policy. The risks of mediated debate, in this view, are that the commercialization of media and politics mean that discussion gets debased into simply another instance of public relations or selling.

There are, however, other approaches to discussion and debate that provide alternative ways of thinking about these matters. The question of a public *sphere* in which rational debate occurs has been partially eclipsed by alternative conceptions of 'publics' (e.g., Latour and Weibel 2005), while the taken-for-granted nature of the economy to be debated has itself been challenged by a greater emphasis on the way that entities such as 'the economy' (or 'markets') are constructed both technologically and discursively (MacKenzie et al. 2008; Çalişkan and Callon 2009). Even terms like 'discussion' or 'debate' have partially given way to a broader concern with controversies and conflicts (Latour 2005; Boltanski and Thévenot 2006; Marres and Moats 2015), and with the question of how certain topics become 'matters of concern' (Latour 2004) in the first place. These developments invite a rather different way of understanding discussion in economic life, in terms of the way that publics congregate around particular issues and topics, their potential to challenge existing institutional definitions of economic issues and problems, and their capacity to endure over time (Callon and Latour 1981; Couldry 2008).

This chapter explores discussion and debate as modes of economic communication and assesses their contribution to economic life – whether in mediated political discussion or everyday conversation. However, while affirming their importance, it also takes seriously insights from actor-network theory and the sociology of conventions that challenge the terms through which we typically think about them. One of the first things we see is that what counts as 'economic' discussion varies according to medium, genre and context – that is, whether we find it on television news, in talk shows, in online discussion forums or in everyday life. At a minimum, these examples make it clear that what counts as 'economic' talk is therefore something that emerges *through* communication, rather than before it. Çalişkan and Callon's (2009) term 'economization' (although not often applied within media and communications) is a useful way of capturing the process by which communicative acts – and particularly those that take on relatively fixed and conventional forms inside media institutions – are part of how 'the economy' is defined.

The sites considered in this chapter also show that dialogue and debate were – as Habermas acknowledged – only ever 'ideal types' of communication and not so easily separable from other communicative acts, such as narrating, advice giving, listening and promoting. This is true not only in the micro spheres of everyday life, where one might perhaps expect to find such overlap, but also in the more formal spaces of political-economic discussion. In some of these cases, discussion is now either so manufactured, or so enmeshed in other types of communication, that it is increasingly hard to justify its elevated or ideal status.

As the chapter moves through its various cases, we also see the salience of other theoretical terms from science and technology studies and actor-network theory. The discussions of economic life that happen on phone-in shows or internet discussion forums, for example, are much better conceived in terms of 'issue formation' and the emergence of temporary and unstable 'publics' than they are in terms of rational-critical debate oriented to understanding (or even to 'success'). These alternative sites for the contestation and (re)formulation of concepts can be powerful opportunities to challenge dominant definitions of the economy, particularly since they tend to think more in terms of Polanyian or Weberian terms of provisioning and making ends meet and are often highly attuned to questions of fairness and justice. Yet as I note in the conclusion, the capacity of these communicative forms to pose an effective challenge is currently limited by their often temporary and unstable nature. This leaves us with an enduring sense of disconnection between the language of economics and 'official' economic debate on the one hand, and the day-to-day discussions of ordinary people on the other.

Mediated discussion about economic life

In media and communication studies, accounts of economic debate and discussion have tended to focus on news programming (for some recent examples, see Berry 2016a; Cushion and Lewis 2017). This near-exclusive attention to news as the principal source of 'economic' content means that the economic discussions that get analysed are of a very particular kind. They are typically limited to the staged interview between a presenter and an 'expert', since relatively few of the flagship news programmes have time for panel discussions with multiple interviewees. Academic studies also tend to focus on the topics covered, and the sources and experts involved, rather than the nature of the dialogue. What is salient about economic debate, in these analyses, is *who* is involved and the kinds of perspectives they represent, rather than the formal properties of the dialogue. As an example of this approach, the Glasgow Media Group's studies from the early 1980s found that economic and political news was typically organized and produced 'substantially around the views of the dominant political group' and that 'the views of those who disagree fundamentally with this position, or who offered alternative approaches, were downgraded and under-represented ... in stark comparison with the careful explanation and heavy emphasis given to the dominant analysis and the political policies [that] flowed from it' (1995: 86). This way of organizing the news, they claimed, was indicative of a particular understanding of economic and social life that upheld the political-economic status quo and saw deviations from it as problematic interruptions. This meant that

> the normal workings of the particular economic system are never treated as if they might themselves generate serious problems. Rather, the causes of economic problems are sought largely in the activities of trade unionists who reject the priorities and purposes of the dominant group. The logic and priorities of the social and economic order thus remain unchallenged. (Eldridge 1995: 86)

It should also be pointed out, however, that studies such as these tend to share with the media organizations they study an acceptance of what 'the economy' consists of. The Glasgow Media Group, for example, relied on established industrial classifications for their analysis (e.g., Eldridge 1995, ch. 5) and focused heavily on industrial disputes and media coverage of union activity. This may have been an understandable concern given the politics of the late 1970s and 1980s, but it was not the only kind of 'economic' activity going on, and it is worth thinking about whose economic experiences, and which kinds of economic activity, were left out by a focus on disputes between bosses and workers. Certainly, more recent discussions about the problems with the measurement of GDP, for example (Coyle 2014), suggest that omissions in what academics measure when they talk about the economy are just as important in constructing common-sense understandings of the legitimate terrain of the 'economic' as media activity. Both media institutions and media academics, in other words, can contribute to the process of 'economization' (Çalişkan and Callon 2009) that determines those aspects that are legitimately part of 'the economy' and those that are not.

This approach to economic discussion – in terms of the types of sources interviewed by news reporters – continues to some extent in more recent work. In the wake of the banking and financial crisis of 2007/8, Berry (2013) examined patterns of source access in UK radio broadcasting, and how these affected the range of debate offered to listeners. His findings indicated that 'City sources dominated the coverage, particularly during the two-week period around the British bank rescue plan', and that the consequences of this were that 'listeners were offered a prescribed range of debate on the UK government's bank rescue plan and possible reforms to the financial sector' (2013: 253), raising questions about impartiality and balance. In two related studies, Berry (2016a, 2016b) examined the kinds of arguments made in the UK press and on the *BBC News at Ten* about the causes of the crisis and potential remedies for the subsequent deficit. Again, he found that 'City experts' – rather than academic economists, who tended to disagree with them – were the largest category, and that 'political and financial elites' dominated coverage, meaning that there was a very limited range of opinion on the implications of the deficit and strategies for reducing it.

These findings are clearly important, not least because the greater space given to what Berry calls 'sectional interests' appears to have had consequences for public understanding. As he points out, at the time of the 2010 election, polling found that 'most people who expressed an opinion blamed Labour for the deficit, saw cuts as unavoidable and thought austerity would be good for the economy' (YouGov cited in Berry 2016b: 557) – all positions typically taken by the 'City sources' whose voices were so widely represented in his study, but which would likely have been disputed by many academic economists. At the same time, it should also be noted that the *form* taken by economic discussion and dialogue is changing: many of the most prominent exchanges on news programmes are not with economic experts or politicians at all, but rather interviews with other journalists. As Tolson (2006: 68) points out, these two-way exchanges between presenter and journalist have in fact come to 'dominate the dialogical possibilities of news'. More importantly, they have consequences for how dialogue proceeds and what economic discussion actually looks like: what journalists do in these 'interviews', Tolson suggests, is very often to simply provide a narrative account of background information about a topic. The conduct of such exchanges is 'very far from the probing cross-examination of public figures with its more or less hostile formulations' (p. 61), and instead is a much more cooperative – and highly staged – effort to invest a story with some narrative drama. At the same time, at least in shorter news bulletins, the voices of politicians, public figures or economic experts are often reduced to mere 'sound bites'.

A related concern about the organization of economic debate on television has to do with the possibility that an ideal of providing a public space for dialogue and debate has been replaced with a simple airing of alternative views. This has sometimes been described in terms of the rise of 'false balance' in public policy discussions. It has become increasingly clear that public service broadcasters in particular sometimes interpret the requirement to be balanced and impartial in their coverage both too narrowly and too literally. This tendency was first identified in relation to science communication, where scientists pointed out that issues on which the scientific community was in virtually unanimous agreement – such as the reality of human-led climate change, or the benefits of vaccination – were often treated in the media as though they were issues of continuing controversy, with two or more evenly balanced 'sides'. This meant that marginal, even crankish, views were given equal billing to those of established scientists. Even when interviewers carefully scrutinized those more marginal views – which was by no means always the case – the sheer fact of giving them equal airtime created the impression that there was more disagreement among 'experts' than was the case. From the perspective of news producers, this approach has the twin virtues of providing 'balance' while also offering a lively debate. On the other hand, it is somewhat disingenuous, and runs the risk of creating doubts in the minds of viewers about whether the benefits of, for example, vaccinating one's children were as clear as they seemed.

A similar issue has arisen in discussion of economic issues. In recent years, there have been two notable cases in the UK – the economic risks of pursuing an 'austerity' agenda in the wake of the banking and financial crisis of 2008, and the economic risks associated with Brexit (i.e., leaving the European Union in 2016) – in which economists have been in overwhelming agreement, but where their views have been presented in television news coverage as matters of great controversy. Some of this can be attributed to a tendency to treat expert knowledge as simply another 'opinion', which can credibly be countered by a non-expert politician who happens to hold a different view. During the EU referendum campaign, for example, most cross-examination of statistical claims during flagship evening news bulletins was made not by journalists or independent experts, but by rival politicians (Cushion and Lewis 2017). Viewers were thus often left with a sense that 'debate' and 'discussion' was a matter of political differences, rather than a question of which statistical claims were accurate and which were not.[1] But another part of the explanation for this tendency has to do with broadcasters' own sense of their role. On the one hand, there are genuine constraints on public service broadcasters: the BBC's editorial guidelines and Royal Charter demand that the BBC be inclusive, and ensure that 'the existence of a range of views is appropriately reflected'. This is a real problem in an age where the range of publicly expressed views is growing all the time, and in which many groups might reasonably claim that their views should be acknowledged (Owen 2018). A further problem is that sectional interests with sufficient money or power can always manufacture a controversy around a topic or policy, even when expert economic opinion is virtually unanimous (see Wren-Lewis 2012). These problems are compounded by the fact that broadcasters often seem to feel the need – and this is perhaps especially true for economic news – to find a big 'story', or controversy, in order to make issues more engaging and appealing to audiences. The combined

effect of these competing demands is that there continues to be an exclusionary quality to economic discussions, given the low levels of economic
literacy for most viewers. In this sense economic discussions on television
news and current affairs programmes not only reproduce dominant ways
of talking about economic issues but also reproduce the stratification of
audiences into those who are, and are not, 'in the know'.

Audience discussion shows

These questions of false balance, or who gets to speak as an economic
expert, are vitally important. Yet, as I have shown, much of the 'discussion'
and 'debate' on news programmes is weak and manufactured, taking the
form of sound bites or staged 'interviews' with journalists. While televised
economic news is quite reasonably a preoccupation for many scholars,
there is arguably more genuine debate about economic issues – as well as
a wider range of understandings of 'the economy' – on radio talk shows
and phone-in programmes, or studio discussion programmes, than on
flagship news programmes. These also attract high audiences, and are
numerous and diverse. For example, LBC, a radio station focused on
'news talk and phone-in speech', recorded 2.78 million listeners in the first
quarter of 2020, which compares quite well with flagship television news
programmes that typically attract between 3.5 and 4.5 million viewers.[2]

Audience discussion programmes have in fact often been held up as
contemporary mediated versions of the eighteenth-century bourgeois
public sphere feted in the work of Habermas and others. Yet as Livingstone
and Lunt (1994) point out, the kind of public sphere that emerges in
television talk shows is not necessarily the one envisaged by Habermas:
instead, it is closer to the oppositional, alternative or radical democratic
public spheres theorized by scholars such as Nancy Fraser, Chantal Mouffe
or Oskar Negt and Alexander Kluge. Rather than offering a model of
rational-critical debate in which 'reasoned consideration of other positions
[...] generate[s] a genuine amendment of original positions in the light
of new arguments' (1994: 26), such shows more often lend themselves to
the expression of diverse or alternative views – including views that may
often be excluded from public discourse – making them more democratic.
Hosts of such shows may actively seek out alternative views (1994: 57), and
the aim is not always to achieve consensus: many talk shows are happy
to leave the studio audience in a state of disagreement. Thus, both the
'point' of debate and the mode of argumentation have been found to be
profoundly different from Habermas's ideal.

Beyond the distinctive model of dialogue and argumentation offered in these shows, the construction of economic life itself is also strikingly different. In Livingstone and Lunt's study, 'economic' discussions were almost never about macroeconomic issues, nor about the sectored economy or particular industries. Instead, they typically related to issues such as poverty or taxation, with an emphasis on the lived experience of audience members. This relates to a point made a number of times so far in this book, that there is a disjuncture between the way that 'the economy' is constructed and understood in news and more formal discursive spaces, and the understandings of economic life that emerge in more everyday sites or (as in the previous chapter) in fictional narratives.

Such shows are also distinctive in the way that authority and expertise to speak about economic issues is constructed. There is a privileging of ordinary people's experiences as real and authentic, which is consistent with the shows' tendency to organize deliberation around the airing of diverse views. Structurally, what this means is that a good deal of the 'discussion' on these kinds of shows comes via the layering of instances of personal narration, which the host then insists that others refer back to. In Livingstone and Lunt's study, an average of ten people – but up to 24 – told personal stories as part of each show; this might be compared with an average of three 'experts' appearing on each show (1994: 107). Elsewhere, Joanna Thornborrow (2007) has shown that the 'arguments' on the talk show *Kilroy* are not discrete linguistic items but in fact 'sequentially emergent from lay participants' narratives', and that it is the combination of narrative and argument that makes such shows distinctive (2007: 1436). This, as she points out, is quite different from traditional models of argumentation, based on 'reason, logic and persuasion' (p. 1438). While the discussions and debates on these audience-led shows often seem more 'real', or more meaningful, than those found in news programming, they do also entail a combination of genres. They contain elements of romance (in the sense of a 'quest' for truth), therapy and self-help as well as political discussion (Livingstone and Lunt 1994).

A corollary of the privileging of ordinary experience is the construction of traditional 'expertise' as just one opinion among many. As Livingstone and Lunt, and other authors, show, 'experts' on audience discussion shows are invariably required to speak to ordinary people's concerns, and if their 'expertise' does not seem to adequately explain or make sense of ordinary experience then its credibility, or at least its practical value, is thrown into question. There is a clear precursor here to contemporary discussions about false balance and, in particular, the concept of a 'post-truth' world (Andrejevic 2013; Davies 2018a). Livingstone and Lunt (1994) show how this privileging of immediate personal experience over expert knowledge means that 'ordinary people become accustomed to making critical comparisons between their own experiences and expert knowledge, [and] to seeing ordinary experiences being accorded time and respect' (1994: 99). They also become used to the spectacle of experts disagreeing with one another, feeding into the perception that direct experience may be a more trustworthy guide. As one audience participant puts it, 'you can always get two experts that disagree with each other' (cited on p. 99). This tendency to question or deconstruct expertise, and to put it into dialogue with ordinary lived experience, is to some extent continued in the forms of online discussion that I explore below.

Online discussion

Another example of mediated discussions about money concerns the deliberations found on social media and in online discussion boards (mentioned briefly in the previous chapter). As opportunities for discussing our economic lives with others in face-to-face contexts (e.g., in banks and post offices) have diminished, other opportunities have emerged in the digital realm. Viewers of shows such as those described above can now engage in discussion with other viewers (and sometimes journalists) via social media. Platforms like Twitter allow people to follow television programmes and debates in real time using hashtags or the @ button, and in doing so, they may contribute their own commentary or discussion online. Such discussions may be highly critical of what is occurring on screen, and may challenge the accounts of the economy and economic life offered by politicians or indeed by other lay commentators. Users may engage in playful behaviour, including irony and sarcasm (D'heer and Verdegem 2014), but there is also evidence that they make substantive contributions to political debates, often pre-empting the discussions that occur between politicians and experts and adding new content of their own (Anstead and O'Loughlin 2011).

Developments such as these suggest that 'discussion' and 'debate' have travelled quite some way from the Habermasian formulation outlined at the start of the chapter. In fact, a better way of thinking about online discussions of economic life may come from science and technology studies and actor-network theory. Here, rather than focusing on what these (often fleeting and incoherent) types of discussion lack, it may be more useful to think of their contribution to the process of 'issue formation' (e.g., Barry 2001; Marres 2007), and to the way that objects or relationships shift from being 'matters of fact' to 'matters of concern' (Latour 2004). This can also be seen in the way economic issues are discussed on internet forums, such as Money Saving Expert (in the UK) or sites for those experiencing debt (e.g., Deville 2016), but also on sites ostensibly organized around other issues, such as parenthood or local community. As with the audience discussion shows mentioned above, these sites are characterized by a discussion of economic issues embedded in everyday concerns, which often bear little direct relation to the emphasis on macroeconomic issues, political economy or economic statistics found in television news. They also typically combine debate and deliberation with other types of utterance such as requests for advice, and forms of personal storytelling and narrative. Online discussions may also be characterized by their scale: debates about economic matters can take on different features, or have different effects, when they extend from a small group of interlocutors in a face-to-face context to a much larger group in contexts of extended mediation and asynchronous communication.[3] Indeed, as the internet has increased opportunities for discussion of economic issues – whether through the comments sections of online newspapers, through social media platforms like Twitter, or the vast number of web discussion boards – there has been a substantial increase in instances of people discussing their economic lives and experiences with strangers in public, perhaps through quasi-anonymous accounts.

How do these extended opportunities for debate shape the ways economic experience can be imagined and understood? In a previous study I considered the case of the UK parenting website Mumsnet and its discussion boards about money and relationships (see Moor and Kanji 2019). Here, participants are invited to initiate, read and respond to discussions about money and finance in the context of close relationships (i.e., those with partners, children, parents, other family and friends). This does not just involve 'discussion' in some abstract sense, but also self-narration and various forms of contextualizing utterance that explain why something is being raised as a matter of debate in the first place. The effect of this is to add a great deal more social detail to our accounts of economic life, and to embed an ostensibly economic experience in something that may not seem 'economic' at all. Narratives take economic questions and calculations that might otherwise seem abstract (e.g., whether partners should always share costs equally), and give them meaning by putting them in the context of specific features of people's lives and relationships. In this way, Mumsnet and similar sites are places where people can 're-embed' economic decisions and calculations into a wider social fabric. As I have noted in chapter 4, such discussions can even cast Mumsnet users as 'publics' who have the ability to define public issues and put them on the agenda of the formal sphere of politics (see Gambles 2010).

In the case of debt discussion forums, contributors are drawn together – and engaged in discussion – around a common concern with indebtedness and how to recover from it. Such forums can challenge normative prohibitions against debt as well as offering practical strategies to recover from indebtedness and resist the aggressive behaviour of debt recovery agencies (see Deville 2016). The case of Money Saving Expert is more wide-ranging, offering discussion boards from subjects that include 'money basics' such as mortgages, credit ratings, bank accounts and insurance, but also issues such as dealing with redundancy, running a charity, and the economic aspects of owning a pet or organizing a funeral.[4] Indeed, despite covering many obviously 'economic' topics like credit cards, mortgages, and so on, the discussions on Money Saving Expert differ markedly from the focus on questions of the macro economy or industry that are the staple of most television news discussions. In addition to threads discussing best deals on insurance, or investment tips for beginners, there are a number of discussions concerned with making ends meet or living within one's means. Here – and indeed across the site – there is a much more widespread concern than one would ever find on the television news with the economy understood in the Weberian or Polanyian sense of householding and provisioning, or the pre-Keynesian sense of 'making economies'.

Online economic discussion, then, is not just abstract 'debating' but also involves the provision of rich contextual detail to explain why a topic matters to a specific person or group and what kinds of concrete features need to be taken into account when discussing it. This means that it involves a variety of additional communicative forms, such as requests for advice, provision of information, narration of one's circumstances and *not* just 'debate' or opinion. As a result, online discussion constructs 'the economy', and economic life, differently than more formal media spaces, and may even be able to contest institutional definitions. 'The economy' – if it is ever discussed in those terms – is not treated as a separate and distinct domain of action, but instead is closely entwined with a range of other social forms related to family, friendship, self-identity, and so on. Furthermore, unlike audience discussion programmes, the topics and discussion threads are usually initiated by users, and there is no 'host' to push people to stay on track. As a result, online discussion about economic matters can range even more freely, crossing and re-crossing the boundaries between domains of action usually established in more formal media spaces.

Everyday discussion of economic issues

Online discussion spaces have by now attracted a fair amount of attention from researchers and, in part because they typically include their own archive of discussions, lend themselves to scholarly scrutiny quite well. By contrast, the apparently 'unmediated' discussions of economic matters that go on in the spaces of everyday life – in homes and shops and workplaces and pubs, for example – are much harder to capture, since they require longer-term and usually ethnographic forms of study. Nonetheless, if we are to understand how economic life is constructed communicatively, and what difference media and mediation make to the forms that 'the economy' takes, it is useful to at least consider the way that more ordinary and unstructured forms of economic speech proceed. Doing so reveals evidence of both similarities and profound differences from mainstream (including mass media) ways of talking about economic issues. They also suggest different terms of reference for assessing 'the economy', grounded in different logics and values.

The most common accounts of 'lay' or everyday economic reasoning tend to come not from ethnographic studies, but from surveys, and sometimes focus groups. Surveys may, however, have significant limitations, since they often effectively 'test' people on their knowledge of concepts from academic economics, particularly macroeconomics, rather than asking them what they *do* know about. Nor do they capture the way that people's knowledge and ideas about economic life appear in dialogue with others, or in more ordinary contexts. Nonetheless, such material usefully highlights the sheer distance between much popular knowledge of economic life and the way that it is talked about in mass media and politics. A survey in the UK in 2015, for example, found a very low level of public understanding of terms like GDP and 'quantitative easing', and confusion between terms like 'debt' and 'deficit' (Inman 2015). A year later, another survey found that only 12 per cent of respondents thought that 'politicians and the media ... talk about economics in an accessible way' (YouGov 2016). This replicates earlier focus group studies of UK viewers watching economic news (Gavin 1998), which found low levels of understanding of an economic news item, with viewers often saying they had only understood the 'gist' of the discussion.

A more interesting example of survey use, which begins to get at what people *do* think about economic matters, is reported by Amariglio and Ruccio (1999): in a study of so-called 'ersatz economics', they describe a survey by the US Advertising Council from the 1970s which left survey questions blank for respondents to write in their own answers. This found that, when free to use their own terms, many respondents described a system ('capitalism', 'free enterprise') rather than a set of concepts. The survey also found that people's responses were often 'personal' or expressed an 'attitude' – again, unlike the language of academic economics. The report's authors also noted that respondents' answers frequently fell outside of any recognizable 'language of economics', and that this tendency was most pronounced among 'low income earners, those in lower level occupations, the old and retired, homemakers, [and] those with low educational attainment', among others. When Amariglio and Ruccio put these findings together with similar studies, they claim that 'ersatz' or 'everyday' economics can be seen as having a distinct and regular discursive structure: first, it 'is often more *declarative* than the economics that is practiced in the academy'. That is, it tends 'to take firm positions on specific economic issues and problems', and it 'emphasizes conclusions – specific observations about economic life, concrete explanations of economic events, advocacy of specific economic policies – instead of a general, scientific way of carrying out economic analysis' (1999: 26). Second, 'concrete actors and agents are seen to make decisions that lead to specific economic events' (p. 26). Third, economic concerns are talked about in terms of the *interests* that are 'associated with, perhaps even served by, economic knowledge' (p. 27). That is, whereas 'academic economists tend to link economic analysis and policy prescriptions either with no interests or with a presumed general interest', for ordinary people the question of interests, and interested-ness, is paramount. Indeed, for many people, 'economic knowledge only has validity, that is, it only makes sense and is worth listening to or reading, if it announces (or at least can be linked to) a specific set of interests rather than hiding behind a presumed disinterestedness' (p. 27).

It should be pointed out that many of the examples mentioned in Amariglio and Ruccio's work do not pertain to discussion or debate as such (although they draw on examples – such as focus groups with high school students – that involved a more deliberative set-up). They are valuable nonetheless because they offer a sense of the language, vocabulary and discursive structure that people draw upon when talking with others in more everyday concepts about economic issues.

A more recent attempt to capture everyday economic discourse, and the deliberative or discursive contexts in which it is embedded, comes from Jack Mosse's (2018) study of the 'economic imaginaries' of a north London housing estate. This study also has the virtue of having something to say about the way that media and mediated ideas about economic life may percolate through into the ordinary 'unmediated' discourse of the estate's residents, even while that discourse clearly had its own interests and preoccupations too.

Mosse's work was based on interviews and observations with residents of the estate. He spoke to people both individually and in groups in the estate's central square, its community centre, its charity shop and the waiting room of the local medical centre. His discussions with groups of residents were particularly revealing in terms of what 'discussion', 'debate' or 'deliberation' – that is, the key terms used by scholars to think about rational democratic discourse – actually look like in everyday contexts. The 'discussions' he observed were more like conversations between friends than the deliberative modes of discourse presumed by communications scholars, with a discursive structure that most closely resembled 'banter' or 'chat'. Economic discussions were deeply imbricated in other non-economic activities of socializing or 'catching up'. When describing a group of women sitting down to mull over the questions he has asked them, he notes that 'sometimes it was like I wasn't there' (2018: 153). And, indeed, it is clear that many of their responses, while apparently deeply felt, could be understood as much in terms of the pleasure of chatting with friends than as part of a more 'serious' deliberative engagement.

One of the most striking findings of Mosse's study is a clear divergence between the taken-for-granted use of the term '*the* economy' (as a self-contained system, or set of indicators of national material wellbeing) in media and political discourse and the lack of recognition of the concept among residents on the estate:

> JM: Ok, and do you feel part of the economy?
> Respondent: No! What do you mean part of the economy?
>
> JM: How would you explain what the economy was to a child?
> Respondent: Haven't got a clue ... (Mosse 2018: 148–53)

It is also notable that on the sole occasion when a respondent is able to engage with Mosse's question, her definition of 'economy' more closely resembles earlier (and more sociological) meanings of the term to do with householding, provisioning or 'making economies' than with the post-Keynesian emphasis on a national or international system:

> JM: Can you remember the first time you thought about the economy as a bigger thing that exists?
>
> Respondent: [...] Thinking about the economy is more thinking about what do I need to live on, what's the minimum I need to spend a week to live properly ... (2018: 145–6)

As discussions proceed, Mosse finds that the most common understandings of the economy and economic life construct them in terms of a power relationship between the advantaged and disadvantaged. As in Amariglio and Ruccio's account, people describe the economy not through a series of concepts but as a system – usually a 'rigged' system, controlled by the rich – from which they were excluded. Many of these concerns seem to emerge from residents' own economic experiences – often of considerable hardship or difficulty – but when asked to account for them, or elaborate on them, Mosse also notes a distinct tendency to reach for topics or explanations that have received wide coverage in UK media. Residents talk, for example, about the consequences of immigration for access to public housing, or about people who take unfairly from the benefits system, as well as the excessive bonuses or executive pay among the very rich (including the expenses claimed by MPs).

What all of this suggests is that what emerges in *discussions* about economic life is often taken, at least in part, from a combination of personal experience and narratives or stories about economic life produced by media institutions. The discussions may reflect people's experiences, but those experiences may be made sense of via narratives and explanations provided by media, rather than through the kind of independent reasoning that notions of 'democratic deliberation' suppose. There are also clearly some continuities between Mosse's findings and what we see in online discussions of economic issues. That is to say, 'the economy' appears in a radically different guise – if it appears at all – in these more everyday forms of conversation and deliberation, and is typically embedded in topics of a more personal and proximate nature. It also covers a more wide-ranging set of concerns and interests than might be found in more mainstream media, and the modes of assessing these topics – what Boltanski and Thévenot (2006) might call their 'regimes of justification' – have more to do with questions of justice or fairness than with the questions of economic efficiency or growth.

Conclusion

How should we evaluate the various types of economic discussion and deliberation found in this chapter, and how far do their differing constructions of 'the economy' matter for public life? Does the category of deliberation and dialogue deserve the elevated status that it has typically held? One thing that is clear from the preceding discussion is that the highest-profile sites for economic discussion and debate are often the most problematic. Television news frequently offers little in the way of real discussion and relies instead on 'vox pops' from politicians and other experts, combined with highly stylized 'interviews' with journalists that are often merely excuses for further description. When news or current affairs shows *do* offer debate, these are frequently plagued by problems of 'false balance' and a perhaps unconsciously felt need to make a dramatic feature out of disagreement. Many broadcasters and publishers have, for diverse reasons, become reluctant to call out factual errors or make their own judgements about where expertise and credibility lies. Finally, what counts as 'the economy' in news and current affairs is often very narrow, with a dominance of macroeconomic news and statistical information, typically presented with little explanation and no account for low levels of audience comprehension or literacy. As such, these sites of potential 'deliberation' tend to reproduce the exclusion of most people from participation in – or even understanding of – economic debate.

As we move away from the news to other sites of dialogue such as audience phone-ins and online discussion forums, economic debate becomes less narrow in its focus and perhaps more closely aligned with the way that economic concerns are perceived and experienced in daily life. It also comes closer to the sociological understanding of economic actions as embedded in relationships, oriented around ultimate values, and concerned with providing for wants and needs. We also start to see – whether on television shows, online discussions or in face-to-face interactions – how economic 'discussion' is typically and regularly blurred with other forms of utterance and genre, such as narrative accounts, self-help and therapy or ordinary chatter and 'banter'. These spaces also reveal the intensely *moralized* ways of framing economic actions and their embedding in social or interpersonal concerns. The economy is often construed in Weberian or Polanyian ways, concerned with 'householding' or making ends meet. We see, in other words, how far discussion is from the Habermasian ideal. Indeed, I have suggested that it may be more useful to think about online 'discussions' of economic life through notions from actor-network theory or science studies – that is, in terms of the definition and contestation of issues (e.g., Marres 2007), and temporary emergence of 'publics' (Latour and Weibel 2005) – rather than in terms of rational debate oriented to consensus formation or rational understanding.

These instances of 'ersatz' or 'everyday' economics (Amariglio and Ruccio 1999) are clearly important areas of study in their own right – not simply as deviations from 'real' economics, nor as deviations from a Habermasian ideal of rational debate. Ersatz economics can be 'transgressive', in Amariglio and Ruccio's terms, because it challenges the technical, abstract ways of conceiving of the economy found in more mainstream academic and other institutional discourses. Whereas academic economists tell stories that are (in their view) mechanical and highly stylized, everyday economics is 'replete with accounts that are historical and anthropomorphic, moral tales that have heroes and villains' (1999: 26). Elsewhere they suggest a range of venues for exploring everyday economics, including 'books and magazine articles written by non-academic economists, editorial columns and newspaper accounts of economic events, discussions on talk shows, the lyrics of popular music, literary texts and visual arts ... and conversations and discussions in a wide variety of social settings, from the dinner table to the shop floor' (1999: 27–8).

While we should not romanticize the everyday discussions of ordinary people – as Mosse's work shows, these may simply rehearse narratives from popular media – they remain important sites of economic conversation, and ones that are all too easily overlooked by the repeated tendency of academic research to focus on flagship news programmes as the main sites where 'economic' issues are discussed. This focus can all too easily reaffirm the idea that 'the economy' is really the macro economy or the financial markets, further entrenching the sense of exclusion felt by ordinary people from economic issues.

What is more, the emphasis on discussion may itself be unhelpful. As John Durham Peters (1999) notes, the elevation of dialogue often tends to overplay its virtues while ignoring the fact that it can be just as tyrannical as other forms of communication (see also Krämer 2015). It also ignores much of the communicative basis of communal life (Carey 1989), and the values inherent in those other forms of communication:

> Life with others is as often a ritual performance as a dialogue. Dialogue is a bad model for the variety of shrugs, grunts, and moans that people emit (among other signs and gestures) in face-to-face settings. It is an even worse normative model for the extended, even distended, kinds of talk and discourse necessary in a large-scale democracy. (Peters 1999: 34)

In the current climate, what is required from mainstream media – and particularly news and current affairs programming – is not so much more simulated 'debate', or the endless fetishization of controversy, but better quality information and a renewed dedication to the educating and informing functions of media. There is already plenty of debate in the world (albeit not of the kind that would satisfy Habermas) – in talk shows, in online discussion forums and in people's ongoing ordinary conversations – and much of it contains the germ of a challenge to dominant (and exclusionary) definitions of the economic. Yet the problem for the more small-scale and 'embedded' forms of economic discussion that I have focused on here is their uncertain capacity to interact with and affect the world of political economy. In Callon and Latour's (1981) terms, they lack the stability and durability to form 'lasting asymmetries' and consolidate power (see also Couldry 2008). What this means, at least for the time being, is a persistent disconnection between the way economic issues are talked about in everyday life and the way they are discussed by politicians and media institutions. I will explore the consequences of this in the conclusion.

Conclusion

We instinctively know that communication is central to our economic lives, and that, in one form or another, it permeates all aspects of provisioning, from conversations in the workplace to online searches for goods and services, and from finding the right savings account to buying gifts for loved ones. Yet when it comes to academic work, we too easily overlook the more mundane communicative aspects of our economic lives – perhaps because they seem so numerous – and focus instead on the biggest or most high-profile instances we can find. Thus, the study of economic communication becomes dominated by 'big' bits of the economy – big business, the financial sector, macroeconomic shifts – or by 'big' forms of communication, such as the outputs of the mass media or the operations of major social media platforms.

There are, however, dangers in treating the more ordinary and small-scale forms of economic communication as though they were trivial or inconsequential. The first is that it obscures the *processes* by which communication comes to make up our economic lives: we tend to look at what is done or said (or not said), rather than whether or how it affects us. The second is that it tends to reinforce media-centrism (Couldry 2006), and takes for granted that media shape our reality – indeed, are the most important force in shaping that reality – without ever having to prove this, and, more importantly, without having to think about how ideas or beliefs circulating at one level of communicative reality (say, the coverage of the financial sector on the 10 o'clock news) sit alongside the values or actions generated at another level of communicative reality (say, discussions about fairness, or deciding how to save for retirement).

The argument of this book has been that the study of economic communication should be fundamentally concerned with the question of how we provide for our material wants and needs, and with how this process gets shared – intentionally or not – with other people, regardless of whether that 'sharing' means companies selling consumer data, or friends talking about pensions in the pub. It certainly must mean more than assessing how the national economy is represented in mass media, and instead must involve looking at how more mundane processes of provisioning are constituted communicatively and socially, including through forms of communication that are considered minor or fleeting, but that collectively add up to a shared reality.

In adopting this perspective, the book has had three main aims: first, to move research on economic communication away from rather narrow understandings of the economy used by (macro) economists and typically replicated in news media, and towards a broader and more sociological category of 'economic life'; second, to shift the focus of research to *communicative practices*, which may or may not be mediated, and away from mass media texts or institutions; and third, to highlight the value plurality in economic life that can be seen when we turn away from dominant genres such as news, or mass media institutions such as television, radio and the press. Part I focused on the way that economic actions *themselves* might be seen as forms of communication, and the very different ways this idea has been taken up inside and outside of economics. Part II examined four varieties of communication – promotion, information, narrative and discussion – that are simultaneously *practices* through which people or institutions attempt to do things with words (Austin 1975) and *constitutive* aspects of our economic lives (Carey 1989).

The advantage of approaching types of discourse is that it can direct us to a wider range of communicative practices than we would normally get when we study economic communication, and to a wider range of media and materials – including no media at all. Trying to think about the sheer range of ways in which economic life is 'narrated', for example, helps us to identify a wider range of actors than just news editors and producers, and leaves as an open question which, or whose, narratives matter most in any given context. The non-media-centric version of media and communication studies that I have outlined matters because it does not assume that *mass* media narratives (or information, or promotion) are more influential than those found in micro media channels or in everyday talk between friends, partners and colleagues. The types of communicative practice I have focused on are necessarily selective and partial, but they point towards an approach to economic communication that would include a wide range of communicative acts, such as advising, teaching, demonstrating, and so on.

Of course, in refocusing the study of economic communication, we must be alert to the fact that ideal types of communication are in reality interwoven with other forms of utterance. We rarely find such pure forms as simply 'informing' or 'discussing', for example. Many instances of economic 'information' are really forms of promotion or discussion, and in practice 'discussing' often breaks down into forms of narrative, advice, persuasion or even self-help. In empirical studies, therefore, it is likely to be more helpful to think about 'mixed messages', and to look at the *layering* of different forms of communication rather than to identify 'types'. Understanding the mixed nature of much economic communication is also helpful in developing a critical approach. It matters, for example, if something is set up as a 'discussion' on television but is really a series of narratives. It also matters if 'storytelling' is really a form of promotion (in the example of 'corporate storytelling' discussed in chapter 5), or if economic 'information' or 'advice' (e.g., from banks) is really a form of self-interested promotion.[1]

Finally, for all of the many advantages of a pragmatic approach to communication, we must also be attuned to the risk of overstating communication's coherence or effectiveness, at the expense of its failures. As John Durham Peters puts it, focusing on communication's instrumental or purposive aspects can 'underplay the strangeness of language' and ignore the vast realm of miscommunication, of 'lost letters, wrong numbers ... and missed deliveries' (Peters 1999: 6). This is not, I think, simply a plea to focus more carefully on audience uses of media – although that is surely important – but rather to understand that more purposive forms of media and communication are themselves situated within a vaster and messier project of 'reconciling self and other' (as Peters puts it) that fails as often as it succeeds.

Reframing communication in economic life

The book has outlined two main ways that media researchers could avoid simply reproducing media or government definitions of the economy. The first is to follow actor-network theorists and others and focus not on 'the economy' as such, but rather on the social processes by which certain activities come to be defined as economic in the first place – what Çalişkan and Callon (2009) call 'economization'. This approach has looked especially closely at the role of economists in making the markets they purport to describe. One obvious route for future communications researchers would be to focus on the communicative construction of 'the economic' by powerful actors, whether economists, media producers (e.g., what gets designated as 'economic' in news and current affairs, and how this is decided) or other institutional actors such as governments, central banks, schools and universities. Indeed, the pedagogical construction of the economy is of particular interest, given the widespread problems of comprehension of economic terms that I have described in the introduction and elsewhere in the book. Many economists have recognized that the undergraduate economics curriculum needs revising, both to capture advances in research and to better reflect real-world complexity. This has led to the creation of an alternative economics syllabus – CORE – parts of which are now included in the economics curriculum of major universities.[2] Elsewhere, sociologists like Fabian Muniesa (2017) have scrutinized the 'case method' of teaching in business schools as a way of understanding how business and economic knowledge is created. All of these developments are worthy of study by communications scholars, and yet media departments only rarely explore pedagogy as a communicative practice, or pedagogical texts as media texts.

Another part of this shift of focus might include analysing how particular *types* of communicative practice construct economic life. I have tried to do this here through a focus on modes of communication and types of discourse, but there has also been interesting work by economists and economic historians on the use of graphs, tables and other figures in representing economic data (e.g., Klein 1995; Blaug and Lloyd 2010; Giraud 2010), while early and important work in this field by Neil Gavin and colleagues (1998) paid attention to the reliance on graphs in economic news. There is scope for much more work in this vein, focusing on the visual culture of economic life. This kind of project might contribute to the concern with forms of inscription and how they circulate (Latour 1990), but it is also consistent with that tradition of media and communications research that focuses on the communicative construction of a shared symbolic world.

A second approach – and the one I have taken up more explicitly here – is to incorporate a more sociological or anthropological definition of economic life into work on media, communication and the economy. This means expanding our definition of the economic to include all processes of providing for material wants and needs (including thinking and talking about them) and focusing on economic action as *meaningful* action rather than 'the economy' as a thing to be represented. Looking at provisioning as an activity, rather than 'the economy' as a thing, means that we draw in many more mundane aspects of economic life, such as shopping, browsing, saving and comparing, as well as discussing, advising, sharing information, and so on. It means not just looking at how powerful actors represent the macro economy in mainstream media channels – important though this is – but also how ordinary people draw on communicative resources of different kinds to provide for their material needs, or make plans for satisfying their wants and preferences.

Shifting focus from dominant conceptions of the economy does not have to mean abandoning critical scrutiny of powerful actors. In fact, turning our attention to the ordinary forms of provisioning associated with online shopping, paying off debts or doing promotional (or self-promoting) work will unavoidably uncover asymmetries of information and imbalances of power, as I have shown in chapters 3 and 4 in particular. Such a shift does, however, mean matching any focus on 'big' actors such as retailers or debt collectors with a corresponding commitment to more mundane aspects of economic communication, and not assuming the centrality or importance of mass media representations (or representations of the macro economy) in shaping people's experiences or worldview.

A reformulated approach to media, communication and economic life also, then, means a shift in the way that media and communications themselves are approached. In the introduction I argued for a decentring of *media* in favour of a broader focus on communication and communicative practice. This is partly because I share the view, most forcefully articulated by Couldry (2006), that 'media-centrism' risks ignoring all the ways in which media do not matter, or are not the centre of people's worlds and viewpoints. To decentre media means, among other things, bringing face-to-face communication – something that is often left to linguists or anthropologists – back within the orbit of media and communications. Doing this allows us to start with the centrality of communication to our economic lives, and then ask what difference media, or mediation, make to it.

As an example of this approach, consider the case explored by Hansen et al. (2018), who assessed the impact of the US Federal Open Market Committee (which makes decisions about monetary policy) releasing transcripts of tape recordings of its discussions to the public. The researchers wanted to see whether making recordings public would have any effect on the deliberative activities of members of the committee. In other words, they took an aspect of economic life in which they knew communication was important, and then tried to assess the difference that mediation made. By comparing two time periods, in which transcripts of the recordings were and were not made available, they identified two types of effects: first, knowing that recordings would be made public led junior members of the committee to be more 'disciplined' in their work. That is, during the 'public' time period they made more effort in preparing for and contributing to meetings, which was reflected in the fact that they spoke across a wider variety of topics and brought more data with them to discuss. Second, however, meetings in general became less 'interactive' after transcripts were published, as well as more 'scripted' and more quantitatively oriented. There was also more conformity from less experienced members, particularly during policy discussions: they made fewer contributions and tended to agree more frequently with the Chair.

What makes this case interesting, from a media and communications perspective, is that it has nothing to do with mass media texts or institutions at all. Instead, it concerns *mediation* – in the form of transcripts of tape recordings – and how this does or does not change the nature and consequences of face-to-face interaction. There are good reasons for media and communications scholars to spend more – or at least as much – time studying these cases of the *mediation* of economic life as they have historically spent on mass media representations of 'the economy'.

While the case explored by Hansen et al. dealt with monetary policy and was able to take advantage of a natural experiment, in my work with Shireen Kanji (2019) – discussed briefly in the previous chapter – I focused on a more mundane aspect of economic deliberation, concerning women's discussions about how money should be treated inside heterosexual relationships. By examining an archive of discussions from an internet forum for mothers, we could explore what happens when such discussions – which already take place in daily life – are subject to the extended mediation of an internet discussion forum. We found not only that women were able to access *more* information than they would otherwise have been able to (about their rights in divorce, for example, but also about other women's lifestyles and choices), but that the extended audiences and interlocutors for their discussions also played a role in the reconstruction of norms about the division of unpaid labour in the home.

What should economic communication be like?

How does the approach taken in this book allow us to make normative claims about what economic communication should be like? For example, what kinds of obligations do large institutions have to their audiences when communicating about economic matters? How do our private troubles in talking about and understanding communication about money relate to public and political histories? The category of economic communication as I have outlined it here is very broad, and seems to preclude hard and fast rules. Nonetheless, I think we can make at least three suggestions about how normative questions about economic communication might be framed.

The first point is simply an observation that most people are already engaged in economic communication – that is, they use communicative resources of various kinds to make sense of and meet their material wants and needs – on a near-daily basis. There does not therefore need to be 'more' economic communication, and there is no reason to think that most people's communication about economic matters needs 'improving'. The question, rather, is about the broader communications environment and how people's ongoing communications about material wants and needs can be acknowledged and supported by the more powerful institutions with which they are entangled. One problem that I have noted in the introduction, and throughout the book, is that the breadth and variety of people's economic lives (including all the ways they talk about them) is not typically reflected in the way that the economy is talked about in more dominant or mainstream sites. A second and related problem is that the way the economy is talked about by politicians and the media is inaccessible to very large proportions of the population, who often do not understand key terms, and say that they find the language of politicians and the media hard to grasp. Mainstream media – such as flagship news programmes – have little time (and sometimes, it seems, little inclination) to address this problem, so the gap between 'insiders' and 'outsiders' persists.

Thus, one of the first ways in which people's communications about their economic wants and needs can be supported is simply by acknowledging this variety and diversity of their economic lives, including the breadth of ways they talk about it. Media outputs of all kinds – from news and websites to novels, films and textbooks – as well as the academic studies that comment on them can be judged according to whether they acknowledge the range of people's economic lives, and their correspondingly diverse ways of talking about them. A second, more specific, issue has to do with the way mainstream news media and politicians *themselves* talk about economic matters. When academics are assessing 'economic communication' in these spaces, they ought to be assessing not only how a news item (or speech or report) is framed and the sources it uses, but also its overall intelligibility to a population that has no educational background in economics. The 'educating' as well as 'informing' roles of public service media ought to be rehabilitated. There is also good reason to think that calls for greater pluralism and criticism in the teaching of economics at universities, as described above, ought to be extended to schools. The current limited attention to 'financial literacy' is mainly aimed at individual decision-making and risk assessment in relation to financial products; in the UK – unlike other countries – economics is not a compulsory subject at school. A meaningful course in economics that not only included heterodox economic thinking but also explicitly put 'economic' questions into dialogue with political and ethical ones (as some university political economy courses do) would be a far better way of supporting people's efforts to formulate and meet their material wants and needs than anything currently available in the school curriculum.

These two suggestions are particularly useful for judging media and cultural outputs, but economic communication also includes the communicative activities of companies and organizations that we either work for or use to access goods and services. Here the questions the book has raised are slightly different, and have more to do with issues of knowledge and information. Chapters 3 and 4, as well as parts of chapter 5, have all drawn attention to our ability to know whether particular communications are strategic or self-interested, as well as to questions of information abundance, information overload and hidden data collection, and how these may shape our economic lives. Thus, a third normative value towards which academic research might orient itself concerns the extent to which particular economic communications advance or restrict our 'right to know' (Schudson 2015). This includes our right to know where messages come from, what they are intended to do, and whether they are factually correct, but it also concerns our rights to know what information is collected about us and how it is stored and used.

One of the reasons why asymmetrical information matters is that public, shared information about our economic lives allows for the creation of community. People's economic communications are part of their social lives, as the longstanding association between 'communication' and 'communion' makes clear (Carey 1989: 18). One of the origins of fixed, public pricing, for example, was the Quaker insistence that all people should be treated equally in the marketplace, regardless of their class or religion (Kent 1990; Moor and Lury 2018), while information about wage levels and benefits allows for collective action against employers and coordinated efforts for change. Lacking information about the economic experience of others (whether the price they pay for goods, or the amount they are paid) makes people vulnerable to discrimination or exploitation, whereas shared information facilitates community and collective action. The much-vaunted 'personalization' of our economic lives, through targeted adverts or 'personalized' prices, should mean more autonomy and freedom for consumers, and an enlargement of their economic possibilities, not more power for companies based on information that they alone can access and use.

As societies face a future that includes new currencies and payments systems, but also privatized data collection and corporations with a near-monopoly hold on certain markets, it is more important than ever to remember that our economic lives are not a separate realm of disinterested calculative activity, but also part of our social lives, and of public culture. Economic action, in other words, is rarely a place where we do battle as individuals, but where – one way or another – we orient ourselves to others. Corporate interests or state institutions may sometimes militate against such collectivities, but our diverse forms of economic communication – from novels to discussion forums, from political speeches to coins – are how we try to make economic action socially and subjectively meaningful. Their variety deserves to be acknowledged.

Notes

Introduction

1 In addition to studies that focus on the reporting of the macro economy, finance, and so on, some scholars have considered the representation of business and entrepreneurship, particularly in 'reality' television formats. See, e.g., Couldry and Littler (2011) and Kelly and Boyle (2011).

2 Coyle is not the first economist to raise questions about the value of GDP, either as a measure of 'the economy', or for understanding economic wellbeing. See Stiglitz et al. (2009), or for a more recent example see Portes (2020).

3 David Graeber (2019) similarly describes the 'near-theological hold' that neoclassical economic thinking has over mass media and public institutions.

4 In *Media, Culture and Society*, for example, of the articles published between 2009 and 2019 more than 500 mentioned 'finance'; only 11 mentioned 'housework'.

5 Contrary to much work in consumer culture studies, Miller argues that the consumption of capitalist commodities is 'hardly ever about individuals and subjectivities' and is more usually motivated by 'the construction of key relationships' (Miller 1998: 194).

Chapter 1: Does *homo economicus* talk? Communication in economic theory

1 Attempts to influence linguistic development range from the low-level prescriptivism of style guides to the existence of 'language regulators' such as the Académie Française, or discrimination and even violence against speakers of minority languages.

2 See Wong (1978) for a discussion.

Chapter 2: The symbolism of money, payment and price

1 Starbucks Stars are the unit of Starbucks' loyalty programme. In 2018, Starbucks CEO Howard Schultz suggested that the company may one day

issue its own digital currency. See Swartz (2020: 139–69) for a discussion of Starbucks' fintech capabilities and infrastructure. The Brixton Pound was a complementary local currency developed in Brixton, south London, in the wake of the 2008 financial crisis as a way of encouraging local trade and support for local businesses. It is currently seeking to develop a tokenized version using blockchain technology (see Algorand 2021).

2 In an interesting variation, Taussig (2010 [1980]) describes the belief among some rural communities in Colombia that a peso bill is occasionally 'baptized' instead of a child. The bill's owner becomes its 'god-parent' and when the bill enters general circulation, 'it is believed that the bill will continually return to its owner, with interest, enriching the owner and impoverishing the other parties to the deals transacted' (2010 [1980]: 126).

Chapter 3: Promotion

1 Habermas acknowledges this difficulty with his concept of 'unconscious deception', which is kind of concealed strategic action (1984: 332).

2 See for example https://www.youtube.com/watch?v=_4S1-W66fF0 and https://www.youtube.com/watch?v=RuAwYsbUq48

3 Personal communication with the author.

4 See Central Banking (2020).

5 For example, in 2015 the Swedish music streaming company Spotify announced that it would offer all staff six months of parental leave on full pay. This was a significant improvement on the legal requirements in both the US and the UK, where it also had employees. Spotify's chief human resources officer said, 'This policy best defines *who we are as a company*, born out of a Swedish culture that places an emphasis on healthy work-family balance [and] gender equality' (cited in Jones and Collinson 2015, emphasis added).

Chapter 5: Narrative

1 The exception is literature departments, where the study of economic themes is well established. See, for example, Woodmansee and Osteen (1999), Delany (2002), Marsh (2007), Poovey (2008), Clune (2010).

2 For an interesting account of how children's stories mediate economic value, see van den Bossche (2017).

Chapter 6: Discussion

1 As BBC presenter Justin Webb noted, viewers were not happy about this state of affairs. They wanted 'to go beyond claim and counter-claim so that they could work out what was true' (cited in Plunkett 2016, n.p.).

2 See Radio Today (2020) and Thinkbox (2020).
3 To give a sense of reach, Mumsnet has approximately 7 million unique users per month and Money Saving Expert has approximately 16 million.
4 See https://forums.moneysavingexpert.com/ for more information about topics covered.

Conclusion

1 In the UK, for example, the distinction between financial 'guidance' and financial 'advice' is highly consequential, since services offering 'guidance' – which in fact refers simply to information – are not regulated by the Financial Conduct Authority.
2 See www.core-econ.org.

References

Abbott, H.P. (2008) *The Cambridge Introduction to Narrative*, 2nd edn, Cambridge: Cambridge University Press.

Abercrombie, N., Hill, S. and Turner, B.S. (1981) *The Dominant Ideology Thesis*, London: Allen and Unwin.

Adler-Bell, S. and Miller, M. (2018) 'The datafication of employment', The Century Foundation. Available at https://tcf.org/content/report/datafication-employment-surveillance-capitalism-shaping-workers-futures-without-knowledge/?agreed=1.

Akerlof, G.A. (1970) 'The market for "lemons": Quality uncertainty and the market mechanism', *Quarterly Journal of Economics*, 84(3): 488–500.

Akerlof, G.A. and Shiller, R.J. (2009) *Animal Spirits: How Human Psychology Drives the Economy and Why It Matters for Global Capitalism*, Princeton, NJ: Princeton University Press.

Algorand (2021) 'Brixton Pound chooses the Algorand blockchain on which to develop a tokenized version of their innovative Complimentary Local Currency, the Brixton Pound', available at https://algorand.foundation/news/brixton-pound-algorand.

Amadae, S.M. (2016) *Prisoners of Reason: Game Theory and Neoliberal Political Economy*, New York: Cambridge University Press.

Amariglio, J. and Ruccio, D.F. (1999) 'The transgressive knowledge of "ersatz" economics', in R.F. Garnett (ed.) *What Do Economists Know? New Economies of Knowledge*, London and New York: Routledge.

Andrejevic, M. (2013) *Infoglut: How Too Much Information Is Changing the Way We Think and Know*, New York and Abingdon: Routledge.

Angrist, J., Azoulay, P., Ellison, G., Hill, R. and Lu, S.F. (2017) 'Economic research evolves: Fields and styles', *American Economic Review*, 107(5): 293–7.

Angwin, J. and Parris, T. (2016) 'Facebook lets advertisers exclude users by race', *ProPublica*, 28 October, available at https://www.propublica.org/article/facebook-lets-advertisers-exclude-users-by-race.

Angwin, J., Varner, M. and Tobin, A. (2017) 'Facebook enabled advertisers to reach "Jew haters"', *ProPublica*, 14 September, available at https://www.propublica.org/article/facebook-enabled-advertisers-to-reach-jew-haters.

Anstead, N. and O'Loughlin, B. (2011) 'The emerging viewertariat and BBC Question Time: Television debate and real-time commenting online', *International Journal of Press/Politics*, 16(4), 440–62.

Antioch, G. (2013) 'Persuasion is now 30% of US GDP: Revisiting McCloskey and Klamer after a quarter of a century', *Economic Roundup*, 2013(1): 1–10.

Ash, J., Anderson, B., Gordon, R. and Langley, P. (2018) 'Unit, vibration, tone: a post-phenomenological method for researching digital interfaces', *Cultural Geographies*, 25: 165–81.

Austin, J.L. (1975) *How To Do Things With Words*, 2nd edn, Cambridge, MA: Harvard University Press.

Ayres, I. and Siegelman, P. (1995) 'Race and gender discrimination in bargaining for a new car', *American Economic Review*, 85: 304–21.

Balint, A. (2016) 'Branded reality: The rise of embedded branding ("branded content"): Implications for the cultural public sphere', unpublished PhD thesis, Goldsmiths, University of London.

Barrett, C. (2019) 'Can Revolut really tell if I've bought a takeaway for one?', *Financial Times*, 8 February, available at https://www.ft.com/content/5c9a7fb4-293e-11e9-a5ab-ff8ef2b976c7.

Barry, A. (2001) *Political Machines: Governing a Technological Society*, New York: Athlone.

Beckert, J. (2011) 'Where do prices come from? Sociological approaches to price formation', MPIfG Discussion Paper 11/3.

Beckert, J. and Aspers, P. (2011) *The Worth of Goods: Valuation and Pricing in the Economy*, Oxford: Oxford University Press.

Beer, D. (2009) 'Power through the algorithm? Participatory web cultures and the technological unconscious', *New Media & Society*, 11(6): 985–1002.

Bénabou, R., Falk, A. and Tirole, J. (2018) 'Narratives, imperatives and moral reasoning', NBER Working Paper 24798, available at http://www.nber.org/papers/w24798.

Berry, M. (2013) 'The "Today" programme and the banking crisis', *Journalism*, 14(2): 253–70.

Berry, M. (2016a) 'No alternative to austerity: How BBC broadcast news reported the deficit debate', *Media, Culture & Society*, 38(6): 844–63.

Berry, M. (2016b) 'The UK press and the deficit debate', *Sociology*, 50(3): 542–59.

Billig, M. (1995) *Banal Nationalism*, London: Sage.

Birch, D. (2014) *Identity is the New Money*, London: Publishing Partnership.

Blaug, M. and Lloyd, P. (eds.) (2010) *Famous Figures and Diagrams in Economics*, Cheltenham: Edward Elgar.

Bollier, D. (2015) 'The blockchain: A promising new infrastructure for online commons', available at http://www.bollier.org/blog/blockchain-promising-new-infrastructure-online-commons.

Boltanski, L. and Thévenot, L. (2006) *On Justification: Economies of Worth* (trans. C. Porter), Princeton, NJ: Princeton University Press.

Borch, C. and Lange, A.-C. (2017) 'Market sociality: Mirowski, Shiller and the tension between mimetic and anti-mimetic market features', *Cambridge Journal of Economics*, 17(4): 1197–212.

Borneman, E. (1976) *The Psychoanalysis of Money*, New York: Urizen Books.

Bourne, C. (2017) *Trust, Power and Public Relations in Financial Markets*, Abingdon and New York: Routledge.

Bradshaw, T. (2012) 'TripAdvisor censured over "trusted reviews"', *Financial Times*, 1 February, available at https://www.ft.com/content/d5dbfb92-4cc7-11e1-8b08-00144feabdc0.

Bramall, R. (2016) 'Tax justice in austerity: Logics, residues and attachments', *New Formations*, 87: 29–46.

Bruner, J. (2004 [1987]) 'Life as narrative', *Social Research*, 71(3): 691–710.

Brunton, F. and Nissenbaum, H. (2015) *Obfuscation: A User's Guide for Privacy and Protest*, Cambridge, MA: MIT Press.

Çalişkan, K. and Callon, M. (2009) 'Economization, part 1: Shifting attention from the economy towards processes of economization', *Economy and Society*, 38(3): 369–98.

Çalişkan, K. and Callon, M. (2010) 'Economization, part 2: A research programme for the study of markets', *Economy and Society*, 39(1): 1–32.

Callon, M. and Latour, B. (1981) 'Unscrewing the Big Leviathan: How actors macro-structure reality and how sociologists help them do so', in K. Knorr-Cetina and A. Cicourel (eds.) *Advances in Social Theory and Methodology*, London: Routledge & Kegan Paul, pp. 277–303.

Carey, J. (1989) *Communication as Culture: Essays on Media and Society*, Boston, MA: Unwin Hyman.

Carey, J. (1997 [1994]) 'Communications and economics', in E. Munson (ed.) *James Carey: A Critical Reader*, Minneapolis, MN: University of Minnesota Press.

Carrier, J.G. (1994) 'Alienating objects: The emergence of alienation in retail trade', *Man*, 29(2), 359–80.

Castronova, E. (2015) *Wildcat Currency: How the Virtual Money Revolution is Transforming the Economy*, New Haven, CT: Yale University Press.

Cawthorne, B. (2016) *A Guide to Brand Storytelling*, London: Butterfly.

Cellan-Jones, R. (2016) 'Blockchain and benefits – A dangerous mix?', BBC News, available at https://www.bbc.co.uk/news/technology-36785872.

Central Banking (2020) 'Communications initiative: Bank of Jamaica', available at https://www.centralbanking.com/awards/4644421/communications-award-bank-of-jamaica.

Chakrabortty, A. (2017) 'One blunt heckler has revealed just how much the UK economy is failing us', *The Guardian*, 10 January.

Christl, W. (2020) Twitter thread, 24 November, available at https://twitter.com/WolfieChristl/status/1331236131447386115.

Clune, M. (2010) *American Literature and the Free Market, 1945–2000*, Cambridge: Cambridge University Press.

Collins, K. (2014) 'Apple trademarks its store layout across Europe', *Wired*, 10 July, available at https://www.wired.co.uk/article/apple-retail-store-trade-mark.

Couldry, N. (2006) *Listening Beyond the Echoes: Media, Ethics and Agency in an Uncertain World*, London: Paradigm.

Couldry, N. (2008) 'Actor network theory and media: do they connect and on what terms?', in A. Hepp, F. Krotz, S. Moores and C. Winter (eds.) *Connectivity, Networks and Flows: Conceptualizing Contemporary Communications*, Cresskill, NJ: Hampton Press, pp. 93–110.

Couldry, N. and Hepp, A. (2013) 'Conceptualizing mediatization: Contexts, traditions, arguments', *Communication Theory*, 23(3): 191–202.

Couldry, N. and Littler, J. (2011) 'Work, power and performance: Analyzing the "reality" game of *The Apprentice*', *Cultural Sociology*, 5(2): 263–79.

Couldry, N., Fotopoulou, A. and Dickens, L. (2016) 'Real social analytics: A contribution towards a phenomenology of a digital world', *British Journal of Sociology*, 67(1): 118–37.

Coupland, N. (2011) 'How frequent are numbers?', *Language and Communication*, 31: 27–37.

Coyle, D. (2014) *GDP: A Brief But Affectionate History*, Princeton, NJ: Princeton University Press.

Coyle, D. (2016) 'The sharing economy in the UK: A report for SEUK', available at http://enlightenmenteconomics.com/the-sharing-economy-uk/.

Coyle, D. (2017) 'Digital platforms force a rethink in competition theory', *Financial Times,* 17 August, available at https://www.ft.com/content/9dc80408-81e1-11e7-94e2-c5b903247afd.

Cushion, S. and Lewis, J. (2017) 'Impartiality, statistical tit-for-tats and the construction of balance: UK television news reporting of the 2016 EU referendum campaign', *European Journal of Communication*, 32(3): 208–22.

D'heer, E. and Verdegem, P. (2014) 'What social media data mean for audience studies: A multidimensional investigation of Twitter use during a current affairs TV programme', *Information, Communication and Society*, 18(2): 221–34.

Dahl, M. (2016) 'People get suspicious when the Uber surge price is a round number', *New York Magazine*, available at http://nymag.com/scienceofus/2016/05/people-get-suspicious-when-the-uber-surge-price-is-a-round-number.html.

Damstra, A. and Boukes, M. (2021) 'The economy, the news, and the public: A longitudinal study of the impact of economic news on economic evaluations and expectations', *Communication Research*, 48(1): 26–50.

Daragahi, B. (2014) 'Isis declares its own currency', *Financial Times*, 13 November.

Davies, J. (2014) 'Our price or your price?', Nesta, available at http://www.nesta.org.uk/blog/our-price-or-your-price.

Davies, W. (2018a) *Nervous States: How Feeling Took Over the World*, London: Jonathan Cape.

Davies, W. (ed.) (2018b) *Economic Science Fictions*, London: Goldsmiths Press.

Davis, A. (2017) 'The new professional econocracy and the maintenance of elite power', *Political Studies*, 65(3): 594–610.

Delany, P. (2002) *Literature, Money and the Market: From Trollope to Amis*, Basingstoke: Palgrave.

Detrixhe, J. and Wong, J.I. (2017) 'Banks are finally preparing to use crypto-currency to move money between them', Quartz, 31 August, available at https://qz.com/1066601/ubss-utility-settlement-coin-could-put-cash-on-a-blockchain-in-2018/?mc_cid=a83b50d216&mc_eid=878e22563a.

Deville, J. (2013) 'Leaky data: How Wonga makes lending decisions', available at https://estudiosdelaeconomia.com/2013/05/20/leaky-data-how-wonga-makes-lending-decisions/.

Deville, J. (2016) 'Debtor publics: Tracking the participatory politics of consumer credit', *Consumption, Markets & Culture*, 19(1): 38–55.

Deville, J. and van der Velden, L. (2016) 'Seeing the invisible algorithm: The practical politics of tracking the credit trackers', in L. Amoore and V. Piotukh (eds.) *Algorithmic Life: Calculative Devices in the Age of Big Data*, Abingdon and New York: Routledge.

Duffy, B.E. (2016) 'The romance of work: Gender and aspirational labour in the digital culture industries', *International Journal of Cultural Studies*, 19(4): 441–57.

Duffy, B.E. (2017) *(Not) Getting Paid To Do What You Love: Gender, Social Media, and Aspirational Work*, New Haven, CT: Yale University Press.

Duranton, G. and Puga, D. (2003) 'Micro-foundations of urban agglomeration economies', NBER Working Paper 9931, available at http://www.nber.org/papers/w9931.

Economist (2015) 'Risk and reward', *The Economist*, 12 March.

Economist (2016) 'Taming the beasts', *The Economist*, 28 May.

Eldridge, J. (ed.) (1995) *Glasgow Media Group Reader, Volume 1*, London and New York: Routledge.

Emmison, M. (1983) '"The economy": Its emergence in media discourse', in H. Davis and P. Walton (eds.) *Language, Image, Media*, London: Basil Blackwell.

Evans, D.S. and Schmalensee, R. (2016) *Matchmakers: The New Economics of Multisided Platforms*, Boston, MA: Harvard Business Review Press.

Fine, B. and Milonakis, D. (2009) *From Economics Imperialism to Freakonomics*, London: Routledge.

Fludernik, M. (2009) *An Introduction to Narratology* (trans. P. Häusler-Greenfield and M. Fludernik), London and New York: Routledge.

Fog, K., Budtz, C., Munch, P. and Blanchette, S. (2005) *Storytelling: Branding in Practice*, Berlin: Springer-Verlag.

Fornas, J. (2012) *Signifying Europe*, Bristol: Intellect Books.

Fourcade, M. and Healy, K. (2007) 'Moral views of market society', *American Review of Sociology*, 33(1): 285–311.

Fourcade, M. and Healy, K. (2017) 'Seeing like a market', *Socio-Economic Review*, 15(1): 9–29.

Freud, S. (1958 [1913]) 'Further recommendations on the technique of psycho-analysis – On beginning the treatment', in *The Standard Edition of the Complete Psychological Works of Sigmund Freud, Vol. XII (1911–1913)* (ed. J. Strachey), London: Hogarth Press.

Freud, S. (1958 [1914]) 'Remembering, repeating and working-through (further recommendations on the technique of psycho-analysis II)', in *The Standard Edition of the Complete Psychological Works of Sigmund Freud, Volume XII (1911–1913)* (ed. J. Strachey), London: Hogarth Press.

Fuchs, C. (2011) *Foundations of Critical Media and Information Studies*, London and New York: Routledge.

Fuller, M. and Goffey, A. (2012) *Evil Media*, Cambridge, MA: MIT Press.

Galloway, A. (2004) *Protocol: How Control Exists after Decentralization*, Cambridge, MA: MIT Press.

Gambles, R. (2010) 'Going public? Articulations of the personal and political on mumsnet.com', in N. Mahony, J. Newman and C. Barnett (eds.) *Rethinking the Public*, Bristol: Policy.

GAO (2009) 'Financial regulation: A framework for crafting and assessing proposals to modernize the outdated US financial regulatory system', GAO-09-216, available at https://www.gao.gov/products/gao-09-216.

Gavin, N. (ed.) (1998) *The Economy, Media and Public Knowledge*, London and New York: Leicester University Press.

Geertz, C. (1973) *The Interpretation of Cultures*, New York: Basic Books.

Gehl, R. (2011) 'The archive and the processor: The internal logic of Web 2.0', *New Media & Society*, 13(8): 1228–44.

Gerrard, J. (2002) 'A sense of entitlement: Vicissitudes of working with "special" patients', *British Journal of Psychotherapy*, 19(2): 173–88.

Gibson-Graham, J.K. (1996) *The End of Capitalism (As We Knew It): A Feminist Critique of Political Economy*, Minneapolis, MN: University of Minnesota Press.

Gibson-Graham, J.K. (2006) *A Postcapitalist Politics*, Minneapolis, MN: University of Minnesota Press.

Gillespie, T. (2014) 'The relevance of algorithms', in T. Gillespie, P. Boczkowski and K. Foot (eds.) *Media Technologies: Essays on Communication, Materiality, and Society*, Cambridge, MA: MIT Press.

Giraud, Y. (2010) 'The changing place of visual representation in economics: Paul Samuelson between principle and strategy', *Journal of the History of Economic Thought*, 32(2): 175–97.

Gleick, J. (2011) *The Information: A History, A Theory, A Flood*, London: Fourth Estate.

Goldhaber, D. (2017) 'Impact and your death bed: Playing the long game', CEDR working paper no. 07242017-1, available at http://cedr.us/publications.html.

Golumbia, D. (2016) *The Politics of Bitcoin: Software as Right-Wing Extremism*, Minneapolis, MN: University of Minnesota Press.

Goux, J.-J. (1990) *Symbolic Economies: After Marx and Freud* (trans. J.C. Gage), Ithaca, NY: Cornell University Press.

Grabher, G. and Ibert, O. (2014) 'Distance as asset? Knowledge collaboration in hybrid virtual communities', *Journal of Economic Geography*, 14: 97–123.

Graeber, D. (2011) *Debt: The First 5000 Years*, Brooklyn, NY: Melville House.

Graeber, D. (2019) 'Against economics', *New York Review of Books*, 5 December.

Guyer, J. (2004) *Marginal Gains: Monetary Transactions in Atlantic Africa*, Chicago, IL: University of Chicago Press.

Guyer, J. (2010) 'The eruption of tradition? On ordinality and calculation', *Anthropological Theory*, 10(1–2): 123–31.

Habermas, J. (1984) *The Theory of Communicative Action, Volume 1: Reason and the Rationalization of Society* (trans. T. McCarthy), Cambridge: Polity.

Habermas, J. (1987) *The Theory of Communicative Action, Volume 2: Lifeworld and System: A Critique of Functionalist Reason* (trans. T. McCarthy), Cambridge: Polity.

Habermas, J. (1989) *The Structural Transformation of the Public Sphere: An Inquiry into a Category of Bourgeois Society* (trans. T. Burger), Cambridge: Polity.

Hall, S. (1977) 'Culture, media and the "ideological effect"', in J. Curran, M. Gurevitch and J. Wollacott (eds.) *Mass Communication and Society*, London: Edward Arnold.

Hall, S. (1984) 'The narrative construction of reality: An interview with Stuart Hall', *Southern Review*, 17: 4–17.

Hansen, S., McMahon, M. and Prat, A. (2018) 'Transparency and deliberation within the FOMC: A computational linguistics approach', *Quarterly Journal of Economics*, 133(2): 801–70.

Hargreaves Heap, S. and Varoufakis, Y. (1995) *Game Theory: A Critical Introduction*, London and New York: Routledge.

Harrington, B. (2008) *Pop Finance: Investment Clubs and the New Investor Populism*, Princeton, NJ: Princeton University Press.

Harrington, D.E. (1989) 'Economic news on television: The determinants of coverage', *Public Opinion Quarterly*, 53(1): 17–40.

Hart, K. (2001) *Money in an Unequal World: Keith Hart and His Memory Bank*. New York: Texere.

Hart, K. (2009) 'The persuasive power of money', in S. Gudeman (ed.) *Economic Persuasions*, New York and Oxford: Berghahn Books.

Hayek, F.A. (1942) 'Scientism and the study of society', *Economica*, 9(35): 267–91.

Hayek, F.A. (1945) 'The use of knowledge in society', *American Economic Review*, 35(4): 519–30.

Hayles, N.K. (1999) *How We Became Posthuman: Virtual Bodies in Cybernetics*, Chicago, IL: University of Chicago Press.

Hayles, N.K. (2006) 'Unfinished work: From cyborg to cognisphere', *Theory, Culture & Society*, 23(7–8): 159–66.

Hayles, N.K. (2012) *How We Think: Digital Media and Contemporary Technogenesis*, Chicago, IL: University of Chicago Press.

Henz, U. and Mills, C. (2018) 'Social class origin and assortative mating in Britain, 1949–2010', *Sociology*, 52(6): 1217–36.

Herrick, J. (2009) *The History and Theory of Rhetoric*, 4th edn, Boston, MA: Pearson Education.

Hewitt, V. (1994) *Beauty and the Banknote: Images of Women on Paper Money*, London: British Museum Press.

Heyman, R. and Pierson, J. (2015) 'Social media, delinguistification and colonization of lifeworld: Changing faces of Facebook', *Social Media & Society*, 1(2): 1–11.

Hickey, S. (2018) 'Open-banking: Radical shake-up, or a threat to your private data?', *The Guardian*, 8 January, available at https://www.theguardian.com/money/2018/jan/08/open-banking-bank.

Hirschman, A.O. (1970) *Exit, Voice, and Loyalty: Responses to Decline in Firms, Organizations, and States*, Cambridge, MA: Harvard University Press.

Hirschman, A.O. (1977) *The Passions and the Interests: Political Arguments for Capitalism before Its Triumph*, Princeton, NJ: Princeton University Press.

Holmes, D. (2014) *Economy of Words: Communicative Imperatives in Central Banks*, Chicago, IL: Chicago University Press.

Inman, P. (2015) 'Lack of financial literacy among voters is a "threat to democracy"', *The Guardian*, 16 March, available at https://www.theguardian.com/politics/2015/mar/16/lack-of-financial-literacy-among-voters-is-a-threat-to-democracy.

Innis, H.A. (1950) *Empire and Communications*, Oxford: Clarendon Press.

Jansson-Boyd, C. (2018) 'How Ikea's shop layout influences what you buy', *BBC Worklife*, available at https://www.bbc.com/worklife/article/20180201-how-ikea-has-changed-the-way-weshop.

Jones, R. and Collinson, P. (2015) 'Spotify to offer staff six months' parental leave on full pay', *The Guardian*, 19 November, available at https://www.theguardian.com/technology/2015/nov/19/spotify-offer-staff-six-months-parental-leave-full-pay.

Julier, G. (2000) *The Culture of Design*, London: Sage.

Kaminska, I. (2017) 'But, but … I thought Bitcoin was supposed to be cheap?', *Financial Times*, 17 March, available at https://www.ft.com/content/9fd8c26e-c28b-324f-8bc5-e50520d5ee55.

Kearney, R. (2002) *On Stories*, London: Routledge.

Kelly, L.W. and Boyle R. (2011) 'Business on television: Continuity, change, and risk in the development of television's "business entertainment format"', *Television and New Media*, 12(3): 228–47.

Kent, S.A. (1990) 'The Quaker ethic and the fixed-price policy: Max Weber and beyond', in W.H. Swatos Jr (ed.) *Time, Place, and Circumstance: Neo-Weberian Studies in Comparative Religious History*, New York: Greenwood Press.

Kinkle, J. and Toscano, A. (2011) 'Filming the crisis: A survey', *Film Quarterly*, 65: 39–51.

Klamer, A. and Leonard, T.C. (1994) 'So what's an economic metaphor?', in P. Mirowski (ed.) *Natural Images in Economic Thought: Markets Read in Tooth and Claw*, Cambridge: Cambridge University Press.

Klein, J. (1995) 'The method of diagrams and the black arts of inductive economics', in I.H. Rima (ed.) *Measurement, Quantification and Economic Analysis*, London: Routledge.

Knight, P. (2013) 'Introduction: Fictions of finance', *Journal of Cultural Economy*, 6(1): 2–12.

Kollock P. (1999) 'The production of trust in online markets', in E.J. Lawler, M.W. Macy, S.R. Thye and H.A. Waker (eds.) *Advances in Group Processes, Vol. 16*, Greenwich, CT: JAI Press, pp. 99–123.

Konings, M. (2015) *The Emotional Logic of Capitalism: What Progressives Have Missed*. Stanford, CA: Stanford University Press.

Kotler, P. and Armstrong, G. (2014) *Principles of Marketing*, 15th edn, Edinburgh: Pearson Education.

Krämer, S. (2015) *Medium, Messenger, Transmission: An Approach to Media Philosophy* (trans. A. Enns), Amsterdam: Amsterdam University Press.

Lanchester, J. (2014) 'Money talks: learning the language of finance', *New Yorker*, 28 July.

Langley, P. (2008) *The Everyday Life of Global Finance*, Oxford: Oxford University Press.

Latour, B. (1990) 'Drawing things together', in M. Lynch and S. Woolgar (eds.) *Representation in Scientific Practice*, Cambridge, MA: MIT Press.

Latour, B. (2004) 'Why has critique run out of steam? From matters of fact to matters of concern', *Critical Inquiry*, 30: 225–48.

Latour, B. (2005) *Reassembling the Social: An Introduction to Actor-Network Theory*, Oxford: Oxford University Press.

Latour, B. and Weibel, P. (2005) *Making Things Public: Atmospheres of Democracy*, Cambridge, MA: MIT Press.

Lee, D. (2019) 'Election debate: Conservatives criticised for renaming Twitter profile "factcheckUK"', BBC News, 20 November, available at https://www.bbc.co.uk/news/technology-50482637.

Levinson, S.C. (2006) 'On the human "interaction engine"', in N.J. Enfield and S.C. Levinson (eds.) *Roots of Human Sociality: Culture, Cognition and Interaction*, Oxford and New York: Berg.

Livingstone, S. (2009) 'On the mediation of everything: ICA presidential address 2008', *Journal of Communication*, 59: 1–18.

Livingstone, S. and Lunt, P. (1994) *Talk on Television: Audience Participation and Public Debate*, London: Routledge.

McClain, N. and Mears, A. (2012) 'Free to those who can afford it: The everyday affordance of privilege', *Poetics*, 40(2): 133–49.

McCloskey, D. (1983) 'The rhetoric of economics', *Journal of Economic Literature*, 21(2): 481–517.

McCloskey, D. and Klamer, A. (1995) 'One quarter of GDP is persuasion', *American Economic Review*, 85(2): 191–5.

McFall, L. (2019) 'Personalizing solidarity? The role of self-tracking in health insurance pricing', *Economy and Society*, 48(1): 52–76.

McFall, L. and Moor, L. (2019) 'Who, or what, is insurtech personalizing? Persons, prices and the historical classifications of risk', *Distinktion: Journal of Social Theory*, 19(2): 193–213.

McGuigan, L. and Manzerolle, V. (2015) '"All the world's a shopping cart": Theorizing the political economy of ubiquitous media and markets', *New Media & Society*, 17(11): 1830–48.

MacKenzie, D., Muniesa, F. and Siu, L. (eds.) (2008) *Do Economists Make Markets? On the Performativity of Economics*, Princeton, NJ: Princeton University Press.

Madianou, M. and Miller, D. (2013) 'Polymedia: Towards a new theory of digital media in interpersonal communication', *International Journal of Cultural Studies*, 16(2): 169–87.

Marres, N. (2007) 'The issues deserve more credit: Pragmatist contributions to the study of public involvement in controversy', *Social Studies of Science*, 37(5): 759–80.

Marres, N. and Moats, D. (2015) 'Mapping controversies with social media: The case for symmetry', *Social Media + Society*, 1(2).

Marsh, N. (2007) *Money, Speculation and Finance in Contemporary British Fiction*, London and New York: Continuum.

Maurer, B. (2012) 'Mobile money: Communication, consumption and change in the payments space', *Journal of Development Studies*, 48(5): 589–604.

Maurer, B., Nelms, T.C. and Swartz, L. (2013) '"When perhaps the real problem is money itself!": The practical materiality of Bitcoin', *Social Semiotics*, 23(2): 261–77.

Menon, A. (2016a) '2016: A review', available at https://ukandeu.ac.uk/2016-a-review/#.

Menon, A. (2016b) 'Uniting the United Kingdom: What comes after Brexit', *Foreign Affairs*, 6 July, available at https://www.foreignaffairs.com/articles/united-kingdom/2016-07-06/uniting-united-kingdom.

Michie, E. (2011) *The Vulgar Question of Money*, Baltimore, MD: Johns Hopkins University Press.

Miller, D. (1987) *Material Culture and Mass Consumption*, Oxford: Blackwell.

Miller, D. (1998) 'Conclusion: A theory of virtualism', in J.G. Carrier and D. Miller (eds.), *Virtualism: A New Political Economy*, Oxford and New York: Berg.

Miller, D. (2001) 'The poverty of morality', *Journal of Consumer Culture*, 1(2): 225–43.

Mills, C.W. (1959) *The Sociological Imagination*, 4th edn, Oxford: Oxford University Press.

Mirowski, P. (1989) *More Heat Than Light: Economics as Social Physics, Physics as Nature's Economics*, Cambridge: Cambridge University Press.

Mirowski, P. (2002) *Machine Dreams: Economics Becomes a Cyborg Science*, Cambridge: Cambridge University Press.

Mitchell, T. (1998) 'Fixing the economy', *Cultural Studies*, 12(1): 82–101.

Mitchell, T. (2002) *Rule of Experts: Egypt, Techno-Politics, Modernity*, Berkeley, CA: University of California Press.

Mitchell, T. (2008) 'The properties of markets', in D. MacKenzie, F. Muniesa and L. Siu (eds.) *Do Economists Make Markets? On the Performativity of Economics*, Princeton, NJ: Princeton University Press.

Montesinos, H. and Brice, B. (2019) 'The era of empirical evidence', working paper, available at https://www.researchgate.net/publication/318600096_The_Era_of_Evidence.

Moon, C. (2013) 'Money as the measure of man: Values and value in the politics of reparation', in M. Cowburn, M. Duggan, A. Robinson and P. Senior (eds.) *Values in Criminology and Community Justice*, Bristol: Policy Press.

Moor, L. (2007) *The Rise of Brands*, Oxford: Berg.

Moor, L. (2018) 'Money: Communicative functions of payment and price', *Consumption, Markets & Culture*, 21(6): 574–81.

Moor, L. and Kanji, S. (2019) 'Money and relationships online: Communication and norm formation in women's discussions of couple resource allocation', *British Journal of Sociology*, 70(3): 948–68.

Moor, L. and Littler, J. (2008) 'Fourth worlds and neo-Fordism: American apparel and the cultural economy of consumer anxiety', *Cultural Studies*, 22(5): 700–23.

Moor, L. and Lury, C. (2018) 'Price and the person: Markets, discrimination, and personhood', *Journal of Consumer Culture*, 11(6): 501–13.

Morley, K. (2017) 'End of fixed prices within five years as supermarkets

adopt electronic price tags', *The Telegraph*, 24 June, available at https://
www.telegraph.co.uk/news/2017/06/24/exclusive-end-fixed-prices-
within-five-years-supermarkets-adopt/.

Mosse, J. (2018) 'Economic imaginaries across the public sphere: An empirical
exploration into economic understandings and representations across
four sites in the UK', unpublished PhD thesis, Goldsmiths, University of
London.

Muniesa, F. (2017) 'The live act of business and the culture of realization',
Hau, 7(3): 347–62.

Nexon, D. (2017) Twitter thread, 24 June, available at http://www.twitter.
com/dhnexon.

Noble, S. (2018) *Algorithms of Oppression: How Search Engines Reinforce Racism*,
New York: NYU Press.

O'Brien, M. (2015) 'Bitcoin revealed: A Ponzi scheme for redistributing wealth
from one libertarian to another', *Washington Post*, 14 January.

O'Dwyer, R. (2015) 'The Revolution will (not) be decentralised: Blockchains',
P2P Foundation.

O'Malley, P. (2009) *The Currency of Justice: Fines and Damages in Consumer
Societies*, Oxford: Routledge.

O'Malley, P. (2011) 'The currency of freedom?', *Social & Legal Studies*, 20(4):
546–56.

Obama, B. (2010) 'Remarks by the President at Laborfest in Milwaukee,
Wisconsin', available at https://obamawhitehouse.archives.gov/
realitycheck/the-press-office/2014/09/01/remarks-president-
milwaukee-laborfest.

OFT (2013) 'The economics of online personalised pricing', OFT 1488, available
at https://webarchive.nationalarchives.gov.uk/20140402154756/http://
oft.gov.uk/shared_oft/research/oft1488.pdf.

Ostrom, E. (1990) *Governing the Commons: The Evolution of Institutions for
Collective Action*, Cambridge: Cambridge University Press.

Otteson, J.R. (2002) *Adam Smith's Marketplace of Life*, Cambridge: Cambridge
University Press.

Owen, C. (2018) 'Why the BBC ties itself in knots over "balance" – Clue:
It's the license fee', The Conversation, 18 July, available at https://
theconversation.com/why-the-bbc-ties-itself-in-knots-over-balance-clue-
its-the-licence-fee-100118.

Pariser, E. (2011) *The Filter Bubble: What the Internet is Hiding from You*, New
York: Penguin.

Parry, J. and Bloch, M. (eds.) (1989) *Money and the Morality of Exchange*,
Cambridge: Cambridge University Press.

Parsons, W. (1989) *The Power of the Financial Press: Journalism and Economic
Opinion in Britain and America*, New Brunswick, NJ: Rutgers University
Press.

Pasquale, F. (2015) *The Black Box Society: The Secret Algorithms That Control Money and Information*, Cambridge, MA: Harvard University Press.

Penfold-Mounce, R., Beer, D. and Burrows, R. (2011) 'The Wire as social science-fiction?', *Sociology*, 45(1): 152–67.

Peters, J.D. (1999) *Speaking into the Air: A History of the Idea of Communication*, Chicago, IL: University of Chicago Press.

Peters, J.D. (2015) *The Marvelous Clouds: Toward a Philosophy of Elemental Media*, Chicago, IL: University of Chicago Press.

Pettinger, L. (2004) 'Brand culture and branded workers: Service work and aesthetic labour in fashion retail', *Consumption Markets & Culture*, 7(2): 165–84.

Phillips, A. (2006) *Side Effects*, London: Penguin.

Plunkett, J. (2016) 'Media should rethink coverage in wake of Brexit vote, says Justin Webb', *The Guardian*, 5 July, available at https://www.theguardian.com/tv-and-radio/2016/jul/05/media-should-rethink-coverage-in-wake-of-brexit-vote-says-justin-webb.

Plunkett, J. and Quinn, B. (2015) 'Telegraph's Peter Oborne resigns, saying HSBC coverage a "fraud on readers"', *The Guardian*, 18 February, available at https://www.theguardian.com/media/2015/feb/17/peter-oborne-telegraph-hsbc-coverage-fraud-readers.

Polanyi, K. (2001 [1944]) *The Great Transformation: The Political and Economic Origins of Our Time*, Boston, MA: Beacon Press.

Poovey, M. (2008) *Genres of the Credit Economy: Mediating Value in Eighteenth- and Nineteenth-Century Britain*, Chicago, IL: University of Chicago Press.

Porter, A. (2011) 'Conservative Party Conference 2011: Defiant George Osborne claims Britain "will ride out the storm"', *The Telegraph*, 3 October, available at https://www.telegraph.co.uk/news/politics/conservative/8804038/Conservative-Party-Conference-2011-defiant-George-Osborne-claims-Britain-will-ride-out-the-storm.html.

Portes, J. (2020) 'Why the government's latest Covid restrictions should horrify economists', *Prospect*, 19 September, available at https://www.prospectmagazine.co.uk/economics-and-finance/why-the-governments-latest-covid-restrictions-should-horrify-economists.

Preda, A. (2009) *Information, Knowledge and Economic Life: An Introduction to the Sociology of Markets*, Oxford: Oxford University Press.

Radio Today (2020) 'RAJAR Q1 2020: London and national brands roundup', available at https://radiotoday.co.uk/2020/05/rajar-q1-2020-london-and-national-brands-roundup/.

Rasmusen, E. (2001 [1989]) *Games and Information: An Introduction to Game Theory*, Malden, MA: Blackwell.

Rivière, J. (1964) 'Envy', in M. Klein and J. Rivière, *Love, Hate and Reparation*, New York: W.W. Norton.

Rochet, J. and Tirole, J. (2003) 'Platform competition in two-sided markets', *Journal of the European Economic Association*, 1(4): 990–1029.

Rona-Tas, A. (2017) 'The off-label use of consumer credit ratings', *Historical Social Research/Historische Sozialforschung*, 42(1): 52–76.

Sanchez-Monedero, J. and Dencik, L. (2019) 'The datafication of the workplace', working paper, available at https://datajusticeproject.net/wp-content/uploads/sites/30/2019/05/Report-The-datafication-of-the-workplace.pdf.

Sandel, M. (2012) *What Money Can't Buy*, London: Penguin.

Schechter, A. (2017) 'Is there a connection between market concentration and the rise in inequality?', *ProMarket*, 5 May, available at https://promarket.org/2017/05/05/connection-market-concentration-rise-inequality/.

Schelling, T.C. (1960) *The Strategy of Conflict*, Cambridge, MA: Harvard University Press.

Schroeder, J.E. (2003) 'Building brands: Architectural expression in the electronic age', in L.M. Scott and R. Batra (eds.) *Persuasive Imagery: A Consumer Response Perspective*, Hillsdale, NJ: Lawrence Erlbaum Associates.

Schudson, M. (2015) *The Rise of the Right to Know: Politics and the Culture of Transparency, 1945–1975*, Cambridge, MA: Belknap Press.

Schwarcz, S. (2009) 'Regulating complexity in financial markets', *Washington University Law Review*, 87(2): 211–68.

Sen, A. (1973) 'Behaviour and the concept of preference', *Economica*, 40(159): 241–59.

Serazio, M. (2013) *Your Ad Here: The Cool Sell of Guerrilla Marketing*, New York: New York University Press.

Shiller, R. (2005) *Irrational Exuberance*, 2nd edn, New York: Broadway Books.

Simmel, G. (1978) *The Philosophy of Money*, London and New York: Routledge.

Slater, D. and Tonkiss, F. (2001) *Market Society: Markets and Modern Social Theory*, Cambridge: Polity.

Sloterdijk, P. (2009) *Terror from the Air* (trans. A. Patton and S. Corcoran), Los Angeles, CA: Semiotext(e).

Smith, A. (1991 [1776]) *The Wealth of Nations*, London: Everyman's Library.

Smith, A. (2010 [1759]) *The Theory of Moral Sentiments*, London: Penguin Classics.

Smithers, R. (2019) 'Flood of "fake" five-star reviews inundating Amazon, Which? finds', *The Guardian*, 16 April, available at https://www.theguardian.com/technology/2019/apr/16/flood-of-fake-five-star-reviews-inundating-amazon-which-finds.

Spang, R. (2015) 'Monetary heterodoxies', *Enterprise & Society*, 16(4): 957–63.

Spang, R. (2016) 'The currency of history', *World Policy Journal*, 33(3): 39–44.

Spence, M. (2002) 'Signaling in retrospect and the informational structure of markets', *American Economic Review*, 92(3): 434–59.

Spillman, L. (2011) 'Culture and economic life', in J. Alexander, P. Smith and R. Jacobs (eds.) *Oxford Handbook of Cultural Sociology*, Oxford: Oxford University Press.

Stäheli, U. (2008) 'Watching the market: Visual representations of financial economy in advertisements', in D.F. Ruccio (ed.) *Economic Representations: Academic and Everyday*, Abingdon: Routledge.

Steedman, C. (1986) *Landscape for a Good Woman*, London: Virago.

Stiglitz, J., Sen, A. and Fitoussi, J-P. (2009) 'Report by the Commission on the Measurement of Economic Progress', available at https://www.economie.gouv.fr/files/finances/presse/dossiers_de_presse/090914mesure_perf_eco_progres_social/synthese_ang.pdf.

Stokel-Walker, C. (2020) 'All the ways Microsoft Teams tracks you and how to stop it', *Wired*, 6 December, available at https://www.wired.co.uk/article/microsoft-teams-meeting-data-privacy.

Storper, M. and Venables, A.J. (2004) 'Buzz: Face-to-face contact and the urban economy', *Journal of Economic Geography*, 4(4): 351–70.

Sunstein, C. (2001) *Republic.com*, Princeton, NJ: Princeton University Press.

Sutcliffe, D. (2017) 'Exploring the darknet in five easy questions', Policy and Internet Blog, http://blogs.oii.ox.ac.uk/policy/exploring-the-darknet-in-five-easy-questions/.

Swartz, L. (2014) 'Gendered transactions: Identity and payment at midcentury', *Women's Studies Quarterly*, 14(1–2): 137–53.

Swartz, L. (2020) *New Money: How Payments Became Social Media*, New Haven, CT: Yale University Press.

Swedberg, R. (2011) 'Max Weber's central text in economic sociology', in M. Granovetter and R. Swedberg, *The Sociology of Economic Life*, 3rd edn, Boulder, CO: Westview Press.

Taussig, M. (2010 [1980]) *The Devil and Commodity Fetishism in South America*, 30th Anniversary edn, Chapel Hill, NC: University of North Carolina Press.

Thier, K. (2018) *Storytelling in Organizations: A Narrative Approach to Change, Brand, Project and Knowledge Management*, Berlin: Springer.

Thinkbox (2020) 'Top programmes report, week 34', available at https://www.thinkbox.tv/research/barb-data/top-programmes-report/.

Thompson, J.B. (1995) *The Media and Modernity*, Cambridge: Polity.

Thornborrow, J. (2007) 'Narrative, opinion and situated argument in talk show discourse', *Journal of Pragmatics*, 39(8): 1436–53.

Tolson, A. (2006) *Media Talk: Spoken Discourse on TV and Radio*, Edinburgh: Edinburgh University Press.

Travis, A. (2006) 'Asylum seekers forced to return to using supermarket vouchers', *The Guardian*, 20 March, available at https://www.theguardian.com/politics/2006/mar/20/immigrationandpublicservices.

Tribe, K. (2008) '"Das Adam Smith Problem" and the origins of modern Smith scholarship', *History of European Ideas*, 34(4): 514–28.

Tufekci, Z. (2015) 'Algorithmic harms beyond Facebook and Google: Emergent challenges of computational agency', *Colorado Technology Law Journal*, 13: 203–17.

Turow, J. (2006) *Niche Envy: Marketing Discrimination in the Digital Age*, Cambridge, MA: MIT Press.

Turow, J. (2011) *The Daily You: How the New Advertising Industry Is Defining Your Identity and Your Worth*, New Haven, CT: Yale University Press.

Vafa, K., Haigh, C., Leung, A. and Yonack, N. (2015) 'Price discrimination in the Princeton Review's online SAT tutoring service', *Technology Science*, 31 August, available at http://techscience.org/a/2015090102/.

Valentine, M. (1999) 'The cash nexus: Or how the therapeutic fee is a form of communication', *British Journal of Psychotherapy*, 15(3): 346–54.

Valentino-Devries, J., Singer-Vine, J. and Soltani, A. (2012) 'Websites vary prices, deals based on users' information', *Wall Street Journal*, 24 December.

van den Bossche, A. (2017) 'Stories of value: The nature of money in three classic British picture books', in A. Mooney and E. Sifaki (eds.) *The Language of Money and Debt: A Multidisciplinary Approach*, Cham, Switzerland: Palgrave Macmillan.

Velthuis, O. (2005) *Talking Prices: Symbolic Meanings of Prices on the Market for Contemporary Art*, Princeton, NJ: Princeton University Press.

von Neumann, J. and Morgenstern, O. (1953) *Theory of Games and Economic Behaviour*, 3rd edn, Princeton, NJ: Princeton University Press.

Walport, M. (2016) *Distributed Ledger Technology: Beyond Block Chain*, London: Government Office for Science.

Walsh, C. (2015) 'Stating support for the city: Thirty years of budget talk', in G. Murdock and J. Gripsrud (eds.) *Money Talks: Media, Money, Crisis*, Chicago, IL: University of Chicago Press.

Waterson, J. (2019) 'Facebook Brexit ads secretly run by staff of Lynton Crosby firm', *The Guardian*, 3 April, available at https://www.theguardian.com/politics/2019/apr/03/grassroots-facebook-brexit-ads-secretly-run-by-staff-of-lynton-crosby-firm.

Weber, M. (1978) 'The nature of social action', in W.G. Runciman (ed.) *Max Weber: Selections in translation* (trans. E. Matthews), Cambridge: Cambridge University Press.

Wernick, A. (1991) *Promotional Culture: Advertising, Ideology and Symbolic Expression*, London: Sage.

Wherry, F. (2012) *The Culture of Markets*, Cambridge: Polity.

Williams, C.L. (2006) *Inside Toyland: Working, Shopping and Social Inequality*, Berkeley, CA: University of California Press.

Wong, J.I. (2016) 'The British government is considering paying out research grants with bitcoin', *Quartz*, 26 April, available at https://qz.com/670708/the-british-government-is-considering-paying-out-research-grants-with-bitcoin/.

Wong, S. (1978) *The Foundations of Paul Samuelson's Revealed Preference Theory: A Study by the Method of Rational Reconstruction*, London and New York: Routledge.

Woodham, J. (1997) *Twentieth Century Design*, Oxford: Oxford University Press.

Woodmansee, M. and Osteen, M. (eds.) (1999) *The New Economic Criticism: Studies at the Intersection of Literature and Economics*, London and New York: Routledge.

Wren-Lewis, S. (2012) 'Policy errors like 2010 austerity – What can academics do?', mainly macro, 18 February, available at https://mainlymacro.blogspot.com/2012/02/policy-errors-like-2010-austerity-what.html.

Yang, Y. (2018) 'China's battle with the "internet water army"', *Financial Times*, 1 August, available at https://www.ft.com/content/b4f27934-944a-11e8-b67b-b8205561c3fe.

Yoshimi, S. (2006) 'Information', *Theory, Culture and Society*, 23(2–3): 271–8.

YouGov (2016) 'YouGov/Rethinking economics survey results', available at https://d25d2506sfb94s.cloudfront.net/cumulus_uploads/document/5tw8cdop65/RethinkingEconomicsResults_160229_Media&Economics_w.pdf.

Zaloom, C. (2006) *Out of the Pits: Traders and Technology from Chicago to London*, Chicago, IL: University of Chicago Press.

Zelizer, V.A. (1994) *The Social Meaning of Money*, New York: Basic Books.

Zelizer, V.A. (2005) *The Purchase of Intimacy*, Princeton, NJ: Princeton University Press.

Zelizer, V.A. (2012) 'How I became a relational economic sociologist and what does that mean?', *Politics and Society*, 40(2): 145–74.

Zuboff, S. (2015) 'Big Other: Surveillance capitalism and the prospects of an information civilization', *Journal of Information Technology*, 30(1): 75–89.

Index